D1059044

# Dreaming in the Dust

*Katherine Chrisman*

# DREAMING
# IN THE DUST

*Restoring an Old House*

Houghton Mifflin Company · Boston · 1986

Copyright © 1986 by Katherine Chrisman

All rights reserved. No part of this work may be reproduced or transmitted in any form or by any means, electronic or mechanical, including photocopying and recording, or by any information storage or retrieval system, except as may be expressly permitted by the 1976 Copyright Act or in writing from the publisher. Requests for permission should be addressed in writing to Houghton Mifflin Company, 2 Park Street, Boston, Massachusetts 02108.

Library of Congress Cataloging in Publication Data

Chrisman, Katherine.
Dreaming in the dust.

1. Dwellings—Remodeling.   I. Title.
TH3401.C47  1986      643'.7        85-21918
ISBN 0-395-38168-1

Printed in the United States of America

Q   10   9   8   7   6   5   4   3   2   1

The author is grateful for permission to quote "The Victorians" by Theodore Roethke © 1963 Steuben Glass, A Division of Corning Glass Works. Commissioned by Steuben Glass for the collection *Poetry in Crystal*.

Portions of this book have appeared in *Metropolitan Home* and *McCall's*.

TH
3401
.C47
1986

J B44023   1.9.87

*For Charlie*

What foul dust floated in the wake of his dreams.

— F. Scott Fitzgerald
*The Great Gatsby*

O the gondolets, the mandolins, the twanging of the lutes,
The girls all dressed in crinolines among the flowers and fruits.
The flowers all symbolical, the lily and the rose,
And how the sherry blossomed on the end of grandma's nose.
The maiden sighs and turns away, the maiden she relents,
Attracted by the glitter of a pile of five per cents.
They danced beneath the arbors, they strolled upon the grass,
O never aware, O never aware of what would come to pass.

— Theodore Roethke
"The Victorians"

Sometimes, as we stare down into the abyss that separates youth from middle age, small cracks open up in our own smooth surfaces, fissures appear, the ground heaves and grows unsteady underfoot. For some people, steam vents release pressure from below; for others, ominous rumblings herald full-scale eruptions in volcanoes dormant for years. One way or another, we make contact with the fires at our centers. This is the mid-life crisis, a sort of aged adolescence in which we rearrange our identities in preparation for the inevitable next stage.

Many of us search for new beginnings at this time. Some people start new careers, others change mates, try new hair colors. Always beneath, the hopeful drum beats, "You *can* begin again. You *can* start over. You *can* have a new life." The search may point to the workings of a true regenerative process, a period of real growth, or merely to the denial of middle age, an effort to preserve the illusions of youth. "There is still time," beats the drum. "The die is not yet cast." Sometimes, if we are lucky, the two are combined: denial leads to growth, and illusions gone, the scales fall from our eyes, and we build anew.

Our new beginning was the purchase of a one-hundred-year-old house. This is the tale of our journey.

# I

# ROSE-COLORED GLASSES

It is November, month of muted colors and pearly light, when I first see the house, and it glimmers as it sits there, square in the middle of its lot, overlooking a mirrorlike lake in the middle of the city, not two miles from downtown. The house looks like a wedding cake, but an old and musty one, left over from a wedding one hundred years ago — Miss Havisham's, perhaps. Mouse eaten, white, three tiers high, brownish areas of rot showing where the mice have dug too deeply, it lacks horizontal accents to set off its vertical masses of white, and it looks out of balance, tipping slightly, as if it were compressed on one side from sitting too long. The house seems to be waiting — waiting either for its death blows or for a new wedding couple to come along with a fresh coat of frosting and a scalpel to sculpt and shear and remold those areas that have crumbled away, to restore it to its former glory as a symbol of a gilded limitless age that never really was.

I don't know on the day when I first see the house that we will be that couple. All I know is that I have fallen in love. The beauty of the house draws me like the proverbial stranger glimpsed across the crowded room, and suddenly I am involved in a whirlwind romance, my head in the clouds. I am in love with the house's balconies, its terraces, its curves; and I am ready to fall in love with such things. Tired of straight angles, rational analytic thinking, I am searching for emotional truths, not rational ones — why people see things the way they do, not whether or not what they see is true. Layers, patterns within patterns, asymmetry, irrationality, idiosyncrasies — these seem to me organic, close to nature, best expressed by curves. Of course, one cannot see around curves, the way one can sight along straight lines, but that seems not to matter when one is in love.

I am in love with the house's floors, banded as they are by interlocking hexagons of beautiful inlaid wood, marquetry, of walnut, birch, and white oak. Thin in some spots, thicker in others, the traffic patterns of a hundred years of moving feet are visible in the joints of the wood. The afternoon I see it, sunlight is streaming through the deep rose and purple stained glass window, with its turquoise fleur-de-lis and green bottle-glass rosettes in the corners, making colored patterns on that astonishing floor. The open stairwell soars a full two stories over the entrance hall. At the top of the stairs, a balcony runs the length of the hall, and there is another stained glass window, a very large half-moon; but it is dark, shingled over on the outside. "How lovely it would look uncovered," I think and, in that instant, unknowingly commit myself to seven years' hard labor.

My husband, Charlie, comes to view the house. I think he will love it too, for though Charlie earns his living as a stockbroker, he is a *bricoleur* at heart; he likes to fix things up —

windows, moldings, lamps, doors and hinges, old brass, old cars. His workshop is outfitted with ninety-seven tiny drawers in three metal chests that hold sorted bolts and nuts and nails and screws. He has planes, saws, screwdrivers, hammers, chisels, wire, glue, paint, sanders, sealers, brass polish. He is prepared for any sort of project, and what is this house, if not one big project?

I remind myself, too, that Charlie is also interested in historic preservation, in fixing something of value that was once beautiful and well constructed, even if it is presently an indefinable mass of metal — like some old cars — that most people would consign to the junk yard. The first time I met him, his dirty fingernails and colored shirt made him stand out against the rest of the party guests like a lone ragweed in a bed of creamy calla lilies, and being more of a thistle than a rose myself, I went right for him. He had been mucking about in oil, dirt, and grease — a natural part, he assured me, of the preservation and restoration of a beautifully constructed, but sadly neglected, 1934 Lincoln limousine. The search for a garage for this fine automobile, and others more recently restored, is one of the reasons that now, fifteen years later, we have encountered this fantastic old house.

He will love it, I think. It fits.

Charlie says nothing as I point out the house's features to him, mentioning the things I like. I show him the window seats, draw word pictures of our children curled up in them, watching the rain, dreaming dreams, reading, cultivating their minds. I show him the balconies, a private one off every room, imagine us sipping café au lait, nibbling on croissants, or greeting the dawn from ours. The views are spectacular, the lake visible from every room. There is a back-yard pool. Two great window bays face the lake from the living room, the window seven feet tall, filling the house with light. "A giant Christmas tree could go here," I say, pointing at the elbow in the rising staircase; but he is muttering, "Walls, eleven feet high; house fifty-two by thirty-six feet; twenty thousand cubic feet of air to heat for each floor; gas at fifty-five cents per cubic foot." He notices the storm windows where the glass has come loose from the frames, the layers of scaly, alligatored paint on the woodwork, the wavy ceilings that indicate breaking plaster within the ceilings themselves. "The keys are coming loose," he remarks, referring to the unstable ceilings where the plaster has separated from the lath. I think he is talking about doors and the need for new locks.

We do not have a meeting of the minds. His answer is a flat no.

The amount of work that has to be done is staggering. The thought of it weighs him down like a boulder on his back. In an effort to lift it off, I adjust some of my visions downward. We will fix it up, preserve only, much as as we fixed up our earlier pre–World War I house. A new coat of paint on the south side, the removal of the metal awning, some chimney work, a few new storm windows to replace the obviously rotten ones, a bit of decorating. We do not discuss restoration at this time. Neither of us even *thinks* restoration.

The word "maybe" begins to creep into Charlie's conversation about the house. He is interested, at least a little. I can feel it. The truth is that we have been looking at houses for the past year and a half. Our younger child, Chris, a kindergartner, lives in a room that to call "cozy" would be euphemistic. It is the size of a walk-in closet. His bed takes up one entire wall, his dresser another, and toys pour out of the closet every time the door is opened. I have caused tears by stepping on two model airplanes within the last week, and one of his shoes has been missing in the jumble for a month. Underneath Chris's room is the kitchen, which is so tight that when the back door is opened, it hits the table. We could push out the back wall for both these rooms, which would make our living space adequate, but we would still lack garage space for Charlie's three old cars. They are currently scattered around the neighborhood in damp rented garages, where mildew and rust from leaks and condensation are rapidly eating them away.

The only question is, will this be the right house for us? It, too, lacks sufficient garage space; but so does every other house that has been for sale in this neighborhood in the past three years. But the lot is oversize; there is room to build.

Charlie has worries, however. He worries about our stamina, our energy, our resources, both financial and physical. I think we have them; but then, I am in love, and lovers are not known for their clear vision. I think we are approaching this thing from a solid groundwork of experience. We did spend five years working on a house that had had no updating for forty years, installing a downstairs bathroom and putting in a modern kitchen. We stripped woodwork in that house, wallpapered and painted, dealt with ice back-up and roof rakes, put on new roof flashing. Also, by working with electricians, Charlie has learned to do some electrical work himself, and I at least know that *Greenfield* and *rock* have nothing to do with pastoral scenes. We *are* experienced, sort of. We have a contractor's rough figure for a repair job, and can handle the cost . . . if we sell our present house.

I am all for putting in a bid right now. The house on the lake has been for sale for two months. The time is right; with winter heating bills looming in the distance, owners are anxious to sell. But Charlie remains unconvinced. The trouble lies in how we look at it. He sees the house as an interesting shell around a ceiling-high stack of projects, all of which will demand his careful attention and hard work. I see it as a dream needing just a little work to make it a reality. We discuss perfectionism and come to the conclusion that it cannot be our goal. We agree to let some things slide.

A warning bell sounds in my brain, but I ignore it. Even the name of one of Charlie's cars, the Peerless, bespeaks his concern for detail and quality. How can I forget the time he wallpapered the ceiling (the *ceiling!*) of our living room and stood there on a scaffold holding up the gooey, paste-covered wallpaper with his head while it refused to stay and draped itself down his back and over his nose and down his front, making him look like Saint-Exupéry's Little Prince after he was swallowed by the snake. All the while, he had this determined look on his face, this certain grim line across his mouth. He was going to get those seams just right even if it took him all night.

But forget I do, because this nineteenth-century house on the lake seems to fit me like a glove. There can be no other. Not only does it have the right number of rooms, the right amount of space, the perfect location, but it fits fantasies I didn't know I had.

I grew up in a house in St. Paul, not too far from downtown, in a neighborhood like this one in Minneapolis. Ours was a nice house. A fine house, really. Red brick colonial, with white trim. Square. No curves. Built in 1907. It did have one balcony, a deck on top of the back porch, but it wasn't a romantic deck, a place from which to greet the dawn. The only thing we ever used it for was early spring sun-tanning with tinfoil held under our chins, trying to outdo those of our classmates lucky enough to be in Florida. Our house was always filled with people, not just our household, which usually numbered seven, but also friends. I don't know whether it was because we had the best chocolate chip cookies on the block, but the door was continually slamming, and batches of cookies disappeared in five minutes. One neighbor boy permanently occupied the TV room. We had water fights, pillow fights, snowball fights. We played kick ball, chicken ball, and baseball outside in the street and in the big back yard. Our house was roomy. There were many good comfortable places for reading or talking. I never noticed the architecture.

It was not my house, but my grandparents', that intrigued me. Built in 1887, it had a turret, which meant that inside there was a curved alcove ringed with velvet window seats, set off from the rest of the living room. Odd bays, a breakfast nook, and other small rooms whose purpose I could only guess were scattered throughout the house. My grandparents' house held secrets and mysteries. The only thing mysterious about my own house was the locked cabinet above my mother's closet where she kept the Christmas presents, and my father's bureau drawer, where he thought he had hidden copies of *Peyton Place* and *The Kinsey Report*. My grandparents' house contained a long, dark-paneled front hall with a stairwell that rose up two stories like the one in the house by the lake. At the rear of the hall was a screened-off area, separated from the rest by pillars and a balustrade, behind which orchestras used to sit and play for parties in my grandparents' younger days. Off this little area was one of the best hiding places for Easter eggs and hide-and-seek — a closet, which contained a safe and a Ouija board. There was talk of séances and lighted candles. My great-grandmother, who had occupied the house before my grandparents, had been a spiritualist. With gum and a string, my aunt had retrieved torn up pieces of paper hidden behind the wainscotting, paper that was covered with scribbles, purported to be automatic writing.

Even the furniture was exotic. Two large, carved, Chinese, ebony chairs, whose arms were dragons' heads with ivory eyes and whose backs were the scaly tails curved around in the forms of lyres, glared at each other over a table. A stiff velvet couch that forced our spines to remain ramrod straight sat opposite a couch so voluptuous and cushiony that rising from it required a helping hand. My great-uncle Allan had died upstairs while sitting on a chair, reading a book that, astonishingly, was open to the page describing the very medical condition that killed him. For years I thought the pillows hidden under the blanket on the bed on the sleeping porch were his body and that he would come back to life at night; and when I spent the night, I cowered happily under the sheets, for this was not really a scary house. It was secure — just mysterious.

Perhaps the mysteries of the house intrigued me so much because of what I took to be the mysteries in my grandmother's character. Like her sofas, she was a woman of contrasts. She could turn her charm off and on like a faucet. When I knew her, she was the personification of propriety. "Young ladies should never sit with their legs crossed," she would admonish. "Cross them only at the ankle, and make sure the right leg is on top, so you can reach for things in a graceful manner," she would say, pausing to reach gracefully for a teacup or a bit of the toasted Norwegian flatbread she favored. At her table, we had finger bowls, and butterballs shaped like tiny golf balls, with indentations stamped on the surfaces. We sat erect, and still, and did not interrupt.

But my grandfather had a gray parrot he had trained to say just one thing: "Go to hell, Claude!" and he refused ever to come to dinner before the end of his favorite radio program, "The Lone Ranger." He used to tease my grandmother by crooking his little finger over his teacup like an eighteenth-century fop, raising it high in a mock salute, then putting it down again so he could dunk his toast in it, all the while urging us grandchildren to do the same thing. And did my grandmother puff up and bristle like a blowfish? No! She rocked with laughter — great, long, booming laughter, as if she, too, had outwitted a priggish schoolmarm — and she would not correct him (or us) at all. In the twenties, my grandparents gave wild parties, so wild that my mother once poured a whole load of expensive bootlegger's whiskey down the sink as a protest. A friend of my grandmother told me about a party guest who had taken out his revolver and shot down the chandelier. Though my grandmother hotly denied this episode, I am sure that it happened. Her denial came purely for the sake of Form, something in which she devoutly believed.

It must have been these memories, along with those of gleaming woodwork, stained glass, carved tiles, and polished balustrades, that triggered my response to the house on the lake, though I wasn't aware of them at the time. There was a sort of echo, an unconscious reverberation, an emotional recognition when I first walked through the front door — and fell in love.

Charlie's grandparents, too, lived in an old house with a turret. He remembers window seats at the end of a long, dark hallway on the second floor; a curved sleeping porch; and green and gold velvet draft-stopping portières at the entrance to the front parlor, which no one ever went into. But this house was in the country, in a farming community in western Minnesota, and Charlie's fondest memories are mostly of the outdoors: of playing in barns, getting water from cisterns, and chopping rhubarb.

Charlie has other connections, other things from the past that link him to old houses, earlier times. His own family's house, in the same neighborhood as the house on the lake, was only twenty-three years old when his family moved into it. But his mother loves old things, as much for the stories they tell as for the objects themselves, and she has filled her house with lovely antiques. A Japanese Imari bowl, bought in Boston to hold punch for Charlie's father's graduation from Harvard in 1916, sits on her piano, just across the room from a carved walnut, barrel-topped desk that had belonged to her Welsh-born father when he was still a bachelor working in a bank in Mapleton, Iowa. In her sun room is a marble-topped Eastlake table that came from Cascade, Iowa, where it had belonged to Charlie's paternal great-great-grandparents. In the dining room is one of a different great-great-grandmother's wedding presents, a very large mahogany Empire bureau. When the family headed for Iowa from Cooperstown, New York, just before the Civil War, the chest, the young wife's most precious possession, came with them in a Conestoga wagon. And when they came to a difficult river crossing in Illinois, and her husband said that the bureau would have to stay behind on the east bank, the young wife folded her arms across her chest, planted her feet, and said: "No. Either it comes with us or I stay here." The bureau crossed the river. For Charlie's great-great-grandmother, that bureau was a reminder, a root, and a tendril stretching back through the miles, giving her solace during those first few years in Iowa — when it was so cold in the winter that the dishtowels froze on the oven door, when it was so lonely that for one year her daughter, Charlie's great-grand-mother, never saw another child.

I remind Charlie of these things, these stories, these connections with the past, as I try to explain to him my love for this old house and my desire to live in it. "Other pieces of the Eastlake furniture from Cascade, Iowa, are still in the attic," he says. "There are a settee, two armchairs, several side chairs. Maybe we could use them — if, that is, we decide to buy the house." I can't believe I am hearing him say these words. He is catching some of my enthusiasm.

The children, too, are eager to move, and they chime in during family discussions. On the first day we looked at the house, Chris, who usually hesitates about new things, always liking to test the water with his toe, settled right into a child-size rocking chair in the third-floor library, took out a book, and said he'd like to stay. Nine-year-old Kate *likes* change, and since we will be staying in the same neighborhood, she doesn't risk losing any friends. She isn't sure, however, that she likes this house. It is so *old*. The floors, to her, look simply dirty, water spotted, gray. She would like a nice wall-to-wall carpet, preferably pink. But she loves the idea of the pool, especially the banana yellow slide. Kate has the dialectical skills of a trial lawyer. In the end, she makes a fine advocate.

Charlie's maybes turn into probablys. He imagines the four of us living here, the children growing into teen-agers in this house. He can see the possibilities for himself — a first-class workshop, his dream garage. How beautiful the eight-inch brass hinges on the dining room door will look when the paint is stripped off, the decorative woodwork once the paint is removed and its indentations and curves are revealed.

But I, who have been so adamant, now start to vacillate. I

pulled out all the stops. I argued, I cajoled, I whined. I stooped to the kind of manipulation I would self-righteously condemn in anyone else. My only saving grace is that Charlie has a history of saying no in a yes voice, and in my heart of hearts, I know he is no pushover. Nevertheless, I fear I have gone too far; so when Charlie says, finally, "Let's do it," I say, "Are you *sure*? Are *you* absolutely sure that this is what *you* want to do? I only want to do it if it's what *you* want to do, too." I say these things over and over, phony that I am, and now it is Charlie who tries to persuade me. He needs to exert only minimal effort.

At the end of November, we take out a loan and sign the papers. We will take possession of the house in January, and move in April, after some of the work has been done. The night we sign, I toss and turn and dream that Chris drowns in the swimming pool. I register him for swimming lessons the next day.

In the beginning of December, we hear about a woman who has some early pictures of the house, and we contact her. Her mother had lived in the house at the time of her marriage, and the pictures are snapshots, taken of the various members of the wedding party, as well as of the house itself. The wedding date was 1894. The woman is glad to show us the pictures, but she does not want them to leave her house; we can copy them there. So one chilly afternoon, camera in hand, we pay a visit to Miss Elizabeth Schutt. The photographs are amazing, and a real surprise. I had imagined the house as having had, originally, a curved porch running around the terrace, with a small Greek Revival–style pediment over the door, similar to what is presently there, but not at all. Instead of the Greek pediment, there is a large portico, a porch really, square, with heavy stone columns. The volume of this porch balances the large front bay and anchors it, eliminating the slight "tilt" I had noticed earlier. It is apparent that the architect had intended something very different from what is visible now.

In the photographs, the contrasting trim is drawn largely in horizontal sweeps of line, again connecting the house to the earth and balancing its vertical thrust. Between the two second-story windows on the front bay is some kind of scrolled decorative work. Strong horizontals frame the area. It makes the present all-white treatment of the front façade look like a blank face with undefined eyes and mouth. The trim adds the definition — the appropriate nose, eyebrows, and eyelashes. Covering the second story are small fish-scale shingles, which give the surface a somewhat rough texture, echoing the rough stone on the first story. It is very different from the present smooth covering of large square cedar shakes.

The house becomes interesting to look at from the outside as well as from the inside. Androgynous, it embodies the feminine in its arcs, curves, balconies, and lightness of detail, and the masculine in its solid stone first story, its heavy stone pillars. The whole first story is built out of large blocks of limestone. And yet, there is nothing heavy about this house. It looks solid and airy at the same time. And it most certainly is not white.

The people in the photographs are wonderful, too. No stodgy Victorians, these, saying words such as "brush" or "bosom" to the camera in order to appear dignified or serene. A wasp-waisted bridesmaid, dressed in yards of white ruffled muslin, leans languidly against an oriental rug. Propped against the wall of the porch are bicycles with giant wheels. A youth nibbling on a blade of grass poses against a pillar. The owners of the bicycles used the porch as a setting for a party; they are

drinking something white, surely not milk, but maybe only lemonade, and they are exchanging hats. A perfect Gibson girl
wears the hat that in another picture graces the head of the
funny-looking man with the big ears. Now bareheaded, he
laughs at his comrade, who wears his visored cap backward,
peak pointing down his back. Those people in the photographs
watched Lake of the Isles being dredged. They raced with
horses on the ice, cut blocks of the frozen stuff to cool their
summer drinks, suffered the panic and bank runs of 1893 and
the silver collapse of 1897, for, like the early 1980s, this was a
difficult period in which to live. The legal abstract for the house
lists at least five owners in the four-year period between 1893
and 1897, the bank having foreclosed on one after another.

Lucky for us, a neighbor has researched all the houses on
the lake for a historic survey, and she tells us that ours is the
second oldest house still standing. She has the names of all the
families who have lived there, from 1887, when it was built by
a Mr. Douglas, who had come from Chicago to start a streetcar
franchise and built on the lot next door to his wife's sister; to
the Pruitts, around the turn of the century; to the Regans, who
occupied the house for the longest time, from 1910 to 1945; to
the Kellys, from 1945 to 1960; to the present owners. Who were
all these people? What were their stories? Miss Schutt tells us
about a peculiar woman who wore funny hats and entertained
male lodgers. Who was she? Interested, we write to descen-
dants of some of these families in an attempt to learn their
histories, and I go to the library to see what I can find by poring
over old newspapers. What I find is hard for me to believe. This
inner-city, most-close-in neighborhood of single-family houses,
this urban park area, where businessmen stroll on their lunch
hours and suburban joggers stop on their way from work to run

the lake's three-mile perimeter, this bustling and lively neighborhood was, one hundred years ago, not even in the city.

In 1887, when Mr. Douglas built his house, there were only 6 houses on the entire lake shore; now there are 117. Lake of the Isles was smaller then, with four islands instead of two, and with the exception of a small area on the east side where our house now stands, the shores were marshy swamps, unfit for human habitation and full of what were thought to be malaria-breeding mosquitoes.

But mosquitoes or not, the lake still drew people, much as it does today. Recreation-minded citizens would take the newly installed streetcar to the Kenwood station, the last stop on the line, to get out of the city, breathe the fresh air, away from coal-burning furnaces, and enjoy nature's amenities — canoeing and bicycling in the summer, horse racing and skating in the winter. A trotting track for sulkies was laid out on the ice in the winter, with an active group, called the Kenwood Driving Club, to run it. Horse racing on the lake was so popular that in 1902 the driving club proposed building a large clubhouse, complete with verandah, on the southwest shore of the lake. The proposal was vetoed in favor of private development, however.

Iceboating drew crowds of people to Lake Calhoun, immediately to the south, though sometimes the interests of the sportsmen clashed with those of commerce. The Minneapolis *Journal* reported a "war" between the owners of the fast-sailing yachts that sped along the ice on runners and the ice cutters, who lifted the blocks of ice from the lake in winter and stored them in ice houses along the shore until they were needed for summer cooling. The sailors were accused of pouring kerosene on the ice to make it unmarketable, the ice cutters of spreading ashes in the paths of the iceboats. The newspaper did not say who won.

The 1880s were boom times for the city of Minneapolis, its population increasing by eleven times in a twenty-five-year period, and Lake of the Isles did not long remain a suburb. The city boundaries pushed closer and closer. The most prestigious new area for development lay just atop Lowry Hill to the north, a short walk away, and the park board acquired a strip of land around the lake, as well as some hilly land to the north. They began the first wave of dredging to build up the shore, anticipating the next push of development in the first two decades after the turn of the century.

By 1905 there were three houses on our block — ours, the relative's next door, and a new one down the street. A canoe dock sat at the foot of Twenty-second Street, just five hundred feet to the north, where now a large pipe releases run-off water into the lake. The owner of our house, Mr. Harold Pruitt — whose construction business was prospering mightily (if not quite honorably) but who still had two years of grace and good fortune left to him before being hit with the three lawsuits that would force him into bankruptcy — was the proud owner of one of the first fifty automobiles in the city. A newspaper photograph taken in 1902 shows him standing next to it, his hand on the fender in a proprietary pose. The car was a four-horsepower steam rig, regarded as the state-of-the-art entry into this new form of sport, whose chief patron was none other than that "most enthusiastic of chauffeurs, King Edward of England."

If Mr. Pruitt's business was prospering, his home life was not. Through an acquaintance, I find and interview Mrs. Hanks, the eighty-seven-year-old woman who grew up in the house to the rear of ours, and she tells me a harrowing tale. When she was a child, she used to hear the neighbors talk about Mrs. Pruitt and her violent temper. The woman was given to sudden and unpredictable rages, during which she would attack her own children. Mr. Pruitt supposedly locked her in a basement room at these times, the room just off the basement stairs. Mrs. Hanks had seen the marks on the door said to be made in Mrs. Pruitt's attempts to escape. She herself, however, had never seen Mrs. Pruitt in any way out of sorts. She remembers an elegant woman, calm and restrained. "Of great gentility," she puts it. But there were rumors. Mrs. Pruitt cared for appearances. Her five children had beautiful manners and were always dressed in spotless white. Mrs. Hanks remembers one Pruitt child, a girl of eight or nine, falling part way into the small goldfish pond in the middle of the garden at the back of the house. Although she had only dampened a foot and an elbow and had gotten a smidgen of dirt on her sleeve, she had been terrified and had run into the house to change her clothes before her mother saw her. Mrs. Hanks would never forget the look of fear on the girl's face. There was definitely something terribly wrong. Mrs. Hanks's own mother had alluded to some wildness in her neighbor's past. "Mrs. Pruitt was very spirited as a young girl," she had said. "It took Mr. Pruitt's steadying hand to calm her down."

Though I shudder, I am pleased with this tale. Maybe our house will have a ghost. If we hear strange noises, we will certainly know where to look. I do hope, though, that other stories will not be so grisly.

And indeed they are not. The next owners of our house, we learn with relief, were happier in the domestic sphere. They were the John J. Regans — owners of a bakery that later grew into a commercial bread business — who bought the house in

1910, a year before the last wave of dredging firmed up the shoreline and made the lake area one of the most fashionable places to live in the entire city. We write to a grandson of this Mr. Regan asking for information, and he sends us some letters and papers pertaining to the house. Two generations of Regans lived here, first the grandfather, then his son. Two generations of Regan children grew up here. One of the letters, written in 1935 by the grandmother (who was living in Omaha) to her son, expressed her feelings about his decision to take the house:

*April 16, 1935*
Are we happy tonight!! Only the dear Lord knows how happy we are to hear you are taking 2405. Your telegram was the cause of great rejoicing between Eleanor, Dad and Mother. . . . I wish you could have been there to see the joy of the three of us when the wire was read. We just stood hugging, all three, and exclaiming, "Oh! Oh!" . . . so happy that the boys can be raised there. [It will be] a wonderful place for boys. What fun skating they will have in winter, and later on maybe a canoe on the lake. Besides, you two have always loved the place. Philomena went there as a bride, and I've always heard her say she would love to have the house, and we are too happy for words! Now Dad and I can die happy that you have 2405! . . . Love to you dears who have lifted a big burden off Dad's and my shoulders. May God bless you. . . ."

Along with the letter came an architect's proposal and a plan for "Tudorizing" our house. When the senior Regans had bought it in 1910, the house was already "old." The majority of new houses springing up around the lake were period revivals — Greek Revival, Georgian Revival, English Gothic Revival, Renaissance Revival, Spanish and Mission Revivals, and especially

Tudor Revival. By the mid-twenties, it was our house that did not fit in with the rest. On a walk around the lake today, I look for what remains of the other nineteenth-century houses on the lake and can find only four of them, all on the east shore, and all virtually unrecognizable as late-nineteenth-century houses. Only their steeply pitched and asymmetrical roof lines give them away. All were given boxy casings of stucco, and two were "Tudorized" in the twenties and thirties, remodeled to make them look like the rest, much as our house was remodeled to give it a fifties look.

I carefully study the architect's proposal for our house. All the porches and balconies are gone. Stucco and fake timbers gird the second and third stories. The beautiful curve of the front bay has been flattened, given right angles. Instead of the plate glass windows that bring the outdoors inside, there are small-paned, leaded glass filters. A diamond-paned oriel window hangs where there was once a graceful balcony. Nothing remains of the wedding cake fantasy. Even the stained glass is gone. Perhaps our house was saved from "Tudorizing" by hard times during the depression, perhaps for some other reason. We may never know. But it seems to me that this house is becoming more than just a house; it is a shelter and a dwelling, a place that has held all the lives that have gone before us, held them as if cupped in a hand, shielding yet enfolding. Here, in this place, history is palpable. Those people — the Regans, the Pruitts, Miss Schutt's mother, the Douglases, and others — slept here, raged here, laughed here, and cried here, and we too are to become a part of all that life; we too will stay for a while within; we too will take our place in the parade and make our own connections with the past and the future.

We begin to acquire a veritable library of books about Victorian houses. A cousin lends us four books. I receive three more as Christmas presents. Soon we own the *Old House Catalogue* and the *Old House Compendium*. We subscribe to the *Old House Journal*. "Have you watched 'This Old House' on TV?" we are asked. We begin to. We read *The Gingerbread Age, American Victorian Architecture, Victorian Houses* and learn why our house is called Queen Anne. We study Downing's and Rookwood's exterior paint colors, read about civic symbolism in neoclassic architecture and how it moved into the nature symbolism that heralded the Victorian age. Doing this research is like exploring the setting for a Victorian novel. We put ourselves into the atmosphere of the house imaginatively, but not yet concretely. It is still abstract, this learning of history. The idea of doing a real restoration has not yet occurred. Nonetheless, we send away for catalogues, begin ordering. We find hinges at an antique shop — little things.

At the same time, we are preparing to leave the house that has been our home for eleven years, and we are dealing with more immediate concerns and problems, like selling the house and packing up our belongings. We entice prospective buyers with the smell of endless pots of steaming cider on the stove, pollen for the bees as it were. We have open houses throughout December — lots of interest, nibbles, but no offers. We even have a showing on Christmas Day, the prospects wading through tissue paper and string, we praying they will not look under the beds and sofas, where there are frantically stowed boxes and half-empty plates. I am unprepared for the strong emotions that go with selling a house that has been a real home. If the buyers are not duly appreciative of the shining brass screws in the window stops that Charlie has spent hours polishing, I decide I don't like them and don't want to sell our house to them. If they question our gas bill, it seems as if they are questioning our integrity. On the other hand, a kindly disposed couple with small children who cannot come up with a quarter of the required down payment almost win me over; but then, if we sell to them, we cannot afford to buy the new house. Finally, after the first of January, we find a family who fits our requirements.

Once we take possession of the house in January and have the freedom to roam through the rooms, we begin to discover hidden treasures: Victorian details and forms hidden behind layers of paint and years of remuddling, details we had not noticed before when we were making the decision to buy the house and could see only the grand scheme. In the basement, we find a Victorian clothespin that still holds some wires (dead ones, thank heavens). Upstairs, in a bedroom closet, an upside-down Victorian match holder substitutes for a missing drawer pull. An old gaslight now holds an electric bulb. One of the three large bedrooms contains a white-painted fireplace. Scratching at it, we find colored glazed tile under the paint. We begin to think about stripping the woodwork. Neighbors have told us about a mystery window, visible from the outside of the house, but nowhere to be found inside. We discover it hidden behind a wall in the dining room and guess that it was covered over in an attempt to camouflage the house's nineteenth-century origins and replace them with the eighteenth-century symmetry more popular in the 1950s, the nadir of appreciation of Victoriana. For this reason also, we think, a wall-size mirror completely covers yet another large stained glass window, this one at the far edge of the dining room. We cannot see the design in this window, however. The whole window is painted over, the design completely covered by thick white paint.

We discover a rose motif that appears in odd spots all over the house. Roses form part of the pattern in the windows — they are in the tile that surrounds the dining room fireplace, and they are carved, in relief, in the wood mantel above. Etched roses are just barely visible in the heavy brass drawer pulls, now painted white, on the drawers below the pass-through between the dining room and the kitchen. Upstairs, in built-in bureaus in the closets, the brass is unpainted, so we can see how the pulls will look when the paint is removed. I wonder who painted the drawer pulls. Was it the Regans? The Kellys, who came later? I'll try to find out. It was certainly the Douglases, the first owners, who chose the rose motif. I am excited about the roses. Roses and lilies were the two favorite symbolic flowers of the Victorian era. There must be lilies somewhere. I can hardly wait to begin the attack with paint remover; lilies are sure to be concealed under the layers of paint.

Charlie has his eye on something he wants to do, too. He wants to put the vestibule back to the way it was. We know the vestibule is wrong. The tiles are big and modern, and several of them are cracked. There would have been a set of inner doors, as in my grandmother's house, to keep the cold air out when someone entered the front door, rather like an air lock on a submarine. Now there are no such doors, and a blast of cold air rushes in whenever the front door is opened. We measure and figure that two 28-inch-wide doors would fill the opening. Someone tells us about a salvage place, and soon we are burrowing around in what looks like someone's grand old attic. Cobwebs hang festooned like garlands from old doors, hundreds of doors — some with glass, some without, square glass, oval glass, round, oblong. Paneled doors, flat doors, doors with carvings and rails, doors that are nothing but two sheets of plywood. But no doors that are 28 inches wide. Charlie is intrigued by a Victorian iron gear with a wooden handle and buys it. "What for? Why?" I ask. Why not? He likes it.

That first hunting trip for old house parts reminds us of the days before children, when we would search through antique shops in old barns, one time uncovering a real find — an old copper boiler, formerly used to wash clothes. Charlie polished and shined it until it glowed and turned it into a wood hopper for the fireplace. Now it holds toys. I go looking for tile, trying to find the small hexagons used in nineteenth-century vestibules. All the old tiles I see are cracked and missing pieces of patterns, but in one expensive store, I discover a modern version from France and bring home a sample — prematurely, as it turns out. We can't tackle the vestibule just yet, not when half the windows are rotten and paint is falling in flakes from the shingles.

Our first major job has to be exterior renovation, and beginning to think about it, we interview several contractors, including a highly recommended young woman who has done some beautiful restorations in an old part of St. Paul. Susan Moore looks far too young to be a general contractor. Slim, with long black hair and the snapping dark eyes and freckles that attest to some wild Celt ancestor, she is the mother of a four-month-old baby girl. She tells me that she became interested in restoration when, as a teen-ager, she helped her family take apart and restore an old farmhouse in Pennsylvania. Later, she and a woman friend built an entire house — from scratch. I am amazed. I find this awesome, unbelievable. I find it easier to accept that her grandfather was a professor of history and that it was from him that she absorbed her love for the subject.

As we walk around the house, she points out some of the

changes that have occurred over the years, changes that we never noticed. The linen closet, for instance, was added in about 1910 and was taken from part of the closet off the bedroom with the painted fireplace. Susan can tell the date by the little row of marching medallions on the edge of the doorknob. Two dingy painted wall fixtures in this same bedroom are really exquisite brass and translucent glass from the earliest days of electricity. The bedroom fireplace once had a second level, whose posts have left barely discernible indentations on the surface of the mantel, which itself has probably been moved from the front hall; the positioning of the tiles indicates a different original mantel. The front vestibule was indeed altered — most likely in the 1950s — two sets of paneled doors removed, and an archway created.

Exploring the basement, we find the remains of the original kitchen behind the furnace, in a dark and forbidding area. The flashlight's beam reveals a recess where there had once been a dumbwaiter to carry the food upstairs to the pantry, now part of the present kitchen. The fireplace in the basement rec room contains blocks of blue limestone that once formed the front porch. Investigations of the basement's chimneys, as well as cuts in the living room floor, show us that our giant living room originally had been two rooms — the traditional Victorian front and back parlors. The front parlor was used only for entertaining important guests and for ceremonies surrounding christenings, weddings, and funerals. The back parlor was rather like the family rooms in today's houses, and ours evidently boasted a diagonal fireplace in a corner, which explains why the marquetry border in the floor stops so abruptly three feet out from the present living room fireplace.

Huffing and puffing, we climb the third-floor stairs in the

turret. The third floor today consists of a main room, a sort of library, carpeted in wall-to-wall red, with bookshelves on three sides; a kitchen area with a sink and small refrigerator; a bathroom; and one bedroom on the front, overlooking the lake. Susan points out that the elaborately carved and crowned corner blocks in the door frames indicate that the third floor was no mere maids' quarters. Definitely not. What we are standing in was once a ballroom. The wall between the main library and the front bedroom is new, again probably 1950s vintage. The ceiling is high, though gabled, reaching eleven feet, at least, at the peaks. Probably underneath the red carpet we will find banded oak floors similar to those in the rest of the house.

Off the former ballroom are three decks, or balconies: a curved one on the front, a sheltered one with a circular moongate on the north, a wide, open one on the south. The guests could have their choice when they needed it. Nothing too crowded. The doors to two of these decks have been altered to window size, but we can still use them to get onto the decks. Maybe we can give a ball here to celebrate the house's centennial.

We go out onto the south deck, which still has a door. Though the temperature is minus ten degrees, it is warm enough here to sit outside. The sun seems to aim itself right at this corner. I think of basking, of tinfoil, of winter tans. Susan starts poking at the large, rough, modern shingles that cover the exterior of the house. "Do you mind if I pull off a few of these?" she asks. "I want to see what is underneath." She removes a few shingles, then a few more. We are rewarded by the best news of all: rows and rows of fish-scale siding. The Victorian shingles are still in place; they have just been covered over by modern siding.

Shortly after Susan's visit, we receive a packet of pictures from the Regan family. They prove to be a gold mine, a source of information we hadn't dreamed existed. The photographs are mostly of interiors, before and after shots, telling the story of the Regans' modernizations in 1910, including the replacement of the gaslights with electricity and the interior decoration, but no structural changes. We can see exactly how the huge living room had once been two rooms with a diagonal fireplace in the back parlor. The woodwork, now painted white, is quartersawn white oak, with beautiful flamelike patterns. Oak paneling, since removed, once fronted the grand staircase, whose balustrade was altered to run diagonally, rather than parallel, to the stained glass window above. The newel post was saved, however; its elaborate carvings of oak leaves and a ridged series of waves reminiscent of those of a Grecian urn attest to its creation at the time when high Victorian was yielding to Beaux Arts decor.

A corner of a fireplace mantel obtrudes from the edge of a photograph of the front hall. We think it is the mantel that is now in Kate's room. Another photograph shows the big dining room stained glass window in all its glory; the quality of the photographs is so good that we can spot a reproduction of Millet's *The Gleaners* at the far end of the room. It is beginning to seem to us that we truly have found a treasure, and that it must be set right, put back the way it was; after all, the house is the second oldest still standing on the lake and the oldest still retaining most of its original features. It is a beautiful example of Queen Anne architecture of some historic importance. We have all these photographs to guide us.

Furthermore, we owe it to the ghost of Mrs. Pruitt. We learn the story of Mrs. Pruitt during our basement explorations.

When Susan and I are looking at the foundations of the chimneys in order to determine the existence of the diagonal fireplace in the living room above, I remember the turn-of-the-century Mrs. Pruitt, who was locked in the room at the foot of the stairs, the very room where we are now standing. Marks were on the door, Mrs. Hanks had said. I examine the door with Susan's flashlight. Old marks *are* there, long, deep grooves — gouges, really — not little dents, as I had imagined, not little hammer marks made by someone shut in for a few minutes during a temper tantrum. This was no *Taming of the Shrew*. These marks were made by raking, clawing — with tools, screwdrivers or chisels or awls, wielded with enormous force. They are horrible to contemplate. The woman who made them was possessed of a fury, of an anger so violent, I can only guess at it. To be locked in like that! It goes beyond reason.

Shaken, I show the marks to a psychiatrist friend. "It's possible she had periods of violence, when she was out of contact with reality, when she would attack her own children, go after them with the same fury that she went after that door," he said. "Remember what the alternatives were at that time. There were no calming drugs. Instead, there were straitjackets. Cold water. Asylums. Maybe it was kinder this way, to confine her until the violence passed."

The image of the woman stays with me for a long time. What could have happened to have driven her to such desperation? What was she like? "Spirited," Mrs. Hanks had said. "Needed her husband's steadying hand to calm her down."

"Spirited," I think. A word applied to horses and women alike. I try to remember what I have read about the ideal Edwardian woman. She was never boisterous or dismally quiet. Always had a pleasant smile for everyone. Never seemed troubled or worried, no matter what the circumstances. Voice low and musical. Full of "laughing cheerfulness, throwing the light of day on all the parks of life," according to the *Journal*. She always had a sunny disposition, and if she was not born with one, she struggled to achieve it. I remember *Anne of Green Gables* and the heroine's efforts, and I think of Mrs. Pruitt and her five children all dressed in spotless white. Such a woman was never allowed to rant and rave and moan and groan, or even suffer in silence. When there was a death in the family, for instance, she had to suffer with a smile on her face, all the while soothing and cajoling her moaning, groaning, ranting, raving husband. She was his emotional servant, expected to bring him consolation in much the same way as she was requested to bring him a cup of tea. She took laudanum.

I remember two pictures I have of my own great-grandparents. The first shows them as newlyweds. They are on a toboggan, just having raced down the big snowy hill in the background. My great-grandmother is laughing; her dark eyes sparkle. In the next photograph, taken fifteen years later, she stands behind her seven children, a hand on the shoulder of the youngest. Buxom now, and severe, she looks as if she knows what duty is. She is stern, her eyes hooded, like a hawk's. A matriarch at thirty-five, she is frowning; a long vertical line bisects her forehead. My great-aunt, her daughter, now eighty-two, once told me that when she was a child, her mother asked her to leave the table when she brought up the subject she had studied that day in school, the reproduction of trees: pine cones, acorns, elm seeds. I think of the woman who was locked in the basement room. Maybe she couldn't take it. How glad I am that I live now, when I can stomp around and wave my arms and let my children play in the dirt.

But Mrs. Pruitt did not retire to her bed, nor did she drift around like a ghost on draughts of laudanum, like Eugene O'Neill's mother. She was violent. This puzzles me. There could have been some cataclysmic event that drove her around the bend. But what? Mrs. Hanks knew nothing about the Pruitts after 1902, when her family had moved away. Inadvertently, we find a clue in the living room floorboards. No inlaid border circles the front half of the living room, the part that was originally the parlor. If there were any room that should have had a beautiful floor, it would have been this one. All the other rooms in the house, even the tiny back bedroom, have these borders — all except our bedroom, that is, and our bedroom is directly above the former front parlor. The floorboards, too, though very old, are joined together in the modern way, each fitting into the next, tongue and groove, unlike the rest of the flooring, which is laid side by side and nailed on the top. So the floors in those two rooms are slightly newer. Why? A fire perhaps? Glowing coals from the corner fireplace spilling out onto the floor? The demented Mrs. Pruitt brandishing a torch? I check the early newspapers for records of fire calls and turn up nothing. I mention the problem to my neighbor who does historic research.

"Well," she says, "there *was* a tornado that came through Lake of the Isles in 1904. It did a lot of damage. I don't recall whether your house was damaged or not, but many on the lake were. You might want to check it out."

Back to the library I go. The Minneapolis *Journal* for August 23, 1904, is full of news about the storm. I read of terrifying events. In one house, "half inch plate glass windows crashed inward, like egg shells, and then powdered and broken fragments of glass were hurled in the air. . . . A wall of water and broken glass rolled through the room and broke against the cowering family." In another, "leaves were forced through

screen doors and plastered on the door behind without losing
their original form, altho' cut to pieces by the mesh of the
screen. Trees were strewn so thick that it was impossible to get
through on foot or with a horse. A rush was made for the livery
stables. . . . Those who did walk home went stumbling over
trees and stepping into gutters filled with water, and in some
places found sidewalks covered for long distances, . . . all to
the accompaniment of exclamatory remarks that might have
offended the prudish, but which echoed the sentiments of
nearly all who heard them Saturday night." One man, "trying
to tie down a cushion on his dock, was thrown out thirty-five
feet into the lake and sank down twice, thinking it was all over
for him. He . . . was then lifted out of the water and a minute
later set back on the shore numb and sore and wondering
whether it were true that he was ashore." Loring and Kenwood
parks sustained terrible damage. "Twenty five years will be
required to repair [it]. All the willows are down. . . ." One man,
an optimist if I ever heard one, suggested that Loring Park had
been too shady, and the storm was a blessing in disguise!

Of our house, there is no specific mention, but there are few
specific mentions of any houses, communications not being
what they are today. In this case, all the telegraph wires were
down, and the paper was forced to rely heavily on unsubstan-
tiated eyewitness accounts. I do read, though, that some houses
on the east side of the lake were badly damaged, "two by their
chimneys being blown in, crashing through to the basement."
In 1904 there were very few houses on the east side of the lake.
The west chimney in our house is directly over the front bedroom and parlor.

As I write this now, there is a "tornado watch" out for the
city of Minneapolis. The air is hot and humid, far too hot and
humid for this early in May and far too abruptly hot and humid

after yesterday's cool temperatures. There is a feeling of closeness and tension, as before a thunderstorm. Although the air around me is still, high above, the clouds are in tumult, turning over and over, the lower layers dark and dirty and moving fast, the mass above lighter and billowing and moving more slowly. An eerie yellowish light makes the lake look bluer than normal, almost turquoise. A tornado is unlikely this early in the year, but if one should appear anywhere in the area, we will have plenty of warning. A civil defense siren will begin wailing, and all prudent people, myself included, will descend to their basements and wait there, preferably huddled against a southwest wall away from any windows, but not under any heavy appliances, until the "all clear" siren sounds.

I was not always a prudent person. Twenty years ago, when I lived for the highs and lows of life (the lows being then more like potholes than pits), I went outside and ran down to the lake after the sound of a tornado siren. The wind was fierce and whipping, bending the trees almost parallel to the ground. It was dark as night, and the rain came down in sheets, but I ran up and down the lake shore, laughing and screaming and exulting at this frenzy of nature, though I could hardly hear myself over the roar of the storm. A huge and menacing black cloud, blacker than charcoal, with ragged edges and dangling wisps, was moving fast toward me underneath the general roiling above. And then I saw it, the funnel, snaking down out of the cloud. It came no lower than a third of the way to the ground, and it moved up and down, as if drawn by an unseen hand, and it passed far, far above me. I learned later that it had flattened all the houses on a peninsula in Lake Minnetonka, sixteen miles to the west, in the space of a few seconds turning them into match sticks, kindling, pickup sticks for giants. Within minutes it had touched down again, on the other side of the city, to the northeast, demolishing a trailer court in the suburb of Fridley and uprooting hundreds of trees. Six people died in that storm twenty years ago. That night I saw their weeping relatives on TV. With my own eyes, I saw the gaping holes where roofs had been and the bare branchless stubs of trees that made the area look like a war zone.

If the chimney did come crashing in through the roof of our house during the tornado of 1904, it must have been like taking a direct hit from a bomb for the Pruitt family. There was no warning siren then. Just suddenly — a vast hole in the roof, the rain pouring in, the tangle of broken pipes and the hiss and smell of escaping gas, the jagged edges of broken floor. Did Mr. and Mrs. Pruitt end up in the basement, I wonder, along with the remnants of furniture, their beds, the parlor set, all buried under piles of sooty bricks? Or were they thrown clear, out into the front yard? How would Mrs. Pruitt have acted under these circumstances, she of the white clothes and perfect manners? Would she have been able to bear it all with a pleasant smile on her face? Without seeming troubled or worried? With a sunny disposition? Or would she have gone berserk, attacking anything within sight?

I think about these things, but I don't have time either to dwell on them or to consider their implications for me and my family. We are much too busy getting ready to move, trying to decide which projects to tackle now, which to postpone until later. We are totally involved in the present; what happened almost eighty years ago seems to have little bearing on our lives today. Mrs. Pruitt's ghost will just have to wait.

Susan Moore comes back for another consultation, a "let's get down to business" type of consultation. It is not so much fun because it is not hidden treasures she uncovers, but potential disasters. "Whether or not you go for total restoration," she says, "it is far wiser to forgo the pretty work, the decorative painting, for instance, and to proceed logically from the roof down — and there is a great deal of work to be done up there around the roof. For starters, both huge chimneys are crumbling and will have to be rebuilt. The roof's overhangs, or soffits, and the fascia boards that decorate them are badly rotted, and the roof will go through only one more winter, and should be replaced now, while the soffits and gutters are being worked on. Squirrels inhabit the house between the third-floor ceiling and the roof; they will be driven out by the activity. You have insufficient insulation. Leaking is occurring in the ceiling over the stairwell; the metal deck above it will have to be replaced; the other decks don't seem to be in such good condition either. Forty-eight of the windows are in bad shape and must have new storms. There is probably some rot in some interior sashes. The balcony railings will have to be replaced; they are falling down. Then, you can think about removing the modern siding, replacing what is rotten in the Victorian fish-scale shingles and decorative work, and paint." We are stunned. Restoration of the front porch we don't even consider at this point. The good news is that the plumbing and electricity are basically okay. The cost estimates are terrible.

"How did we get into this mess?"

"Let's consider this *calmly*."

"What if we don't do it?"

During this period of questioning and indecision, we embark on three interior remodeling projects we want to complete before we move in. We will be living in the house while the *exterior* work is going on. The workmen and the dust will be outside, we think, and not too disturbing to us inhabitants, who can stay safe and warm and dry and comfortable inside, once these small interior jobs are finished. We are very astute and wise, I think — good planners.

The first job is a minor kitchen remodeling — mostly cosmetic — a slight rearrangement of the existing cabinets, the addition of a peninsula counter, a new floor. Susan points out, however, that the ceiling has been lowered by more than a foot and a half, and if we are thinking in terms of restoration at all, it will make sense to raise it back to its original height. She has also noticed that all the window casings have been removed; they will have to be recreated. We listen without digesting this new information and hire a carpenter, still thinking of the kitchen work as a very minor job.

Our second project is the refurbishing of a bedroom for Kate. Of the two children, she cares most about how her room looks, and we think that having a finished bedroom that she can help decorate will enable her to respond more favorably to the house. She wanted the larger of the two children's bedrooms, but Chris, who has been deprived for so long, will get it. As compensation, her room will be the first to be fixed up. Although Chris is happy with the idea of having a big room, he is not quite able to visualize himself in it and hesitates to leave his little den. He voices his uncertainty in pleas that he not be separated from his own bed, not even for one night. We assure him that his bed will travel with him. His bed is like a security blanket, something safe that he knows and can deal with. Chris has always been the kind of child who needs to master something before he feels comfortable with it. When he learned to walk, for instance, he did it not by trial and error, taking a few steps and falling and trying again and again. Instead, he took a few steps, fell, and didn't try again for four months, when he stood up one day and simply walked away. When he was four, he took up the subject of dinosaurs. He would read books only about dinosaurs and refused to read anything else. He learned all their names: stegosaurus, brontosaurus, triceratops, the turtlelike ankylosaurus, the fierce tyrannosaurus. Next it was airplanes, World War I, World War II, Fokkers, Messerschmitts, Sopwith Camels, B-27s, B-29s, 727s, 747s, DC-10s — he can tell them apart when they fly overhead. Now he has taken up model making. He can "read" a diagram I can only guess at, and when he needs help, he has the answer figured out before I can tell which way is up. If past performance is any guide, there will soon be so many model airplanes hanging from his ceiling that we will be brushing them away from our faces like gnats.

Kate, on the other hand, is a plunger. She does not worry at all about learning to swim before she heads for deep water. Literally. When she was very young, I used to spend my days at the beach, not sunning and chatting like the other mothers, but standing knee deep in the water, because, like a lemming, she always headed out to sea. Now, at almost nine, she is savvy and fearless. She will do things that would intimidate most of her friends, such as calling an adult to ask for directions to a place she wants to visit and then instructing our babysitter how to get there. She is something of a leader among her friends, and she has already developed a strong sense of style. It is important to her to be up-to-date and in fashion, and this is another reason for doing her room first and letting her choose the wallpaper. Her room contains the door to the second-floor sleeping porch and has its very own fireplace. I tell her she can make up spooky stories for her friends on sleepovers and give performances and puppet shows on the back porch. Kate's ambition in life is to be a star. She puts on Punch and Judy shows with lots of banging heads and has a few magician's tricks in her repertoire, but her favorite performance is that of the dying swan in *Swan Lake*, which she makes truly pathetic, her head hanging to the side and her hands folded on her chest over the pink satin tutu, as she imagines how sad it is for everyone to see her breathe her last. The back porch is a perfect stage. Here she can perform to the world below. It is like a giant puppet theater. Later on she can play Juliet.

We plan to strip the woodwork in Kate's bedroom, in order to see how much time and effort it will involve, because we are entertaining tentative notions of stripping the whole downstairs. The woodwork in Kate's room consists of casings for three windows and three doors, a foot-high floor molding with eight beads and a curve, and the painted fireplace. The corner blocks on the windows and doors, as in the rest of the house, are of the Eastlake period, with carved inset rosettes and spoon-carved crowns and corners. These corner blocks are part of what attracted me to the house in the first place. They have exactly the same designs as the old furniture on a Wisconsin farm I loved as a child. Their features have been blurred by seventy years' accumulation of paint, and we are curious to see what the blocks will look like with the paint removed.

We begin spending every weekend, and many evenings as well, working with paint remover and heat gun. We also hire a high school boy to help on weekends and some afternoons after school, and some days all five of us work on it together, the children and I at the fireplace, mucking about in paint remover, Charlie and Ward on the heat guns. We scorch; we gouge; we track clumps of newspaper soggy with paint remover through the house. We get it in our fingers, in our eyes, and repeatedly run to the bathroom to flush out some stinging skin. We listen to every opera the Met performs that winter and, in dithering moments, compose a few of our own. We take the corner blocks off and soak them in paint remover, then attack them with tools scrounged from our dentist. It takes three hours to remove the paint from each corner block. Charlie eventually dismantles the fireplace. We simply can't get the paint out of the cracks and carvings while it is intact. The tiles turn out to be a combination of pretty green, dark red, and dark yellow — very Victorian — and entirely glazed.

It takes us more than two months to strip the woodwork in that one room, and we are within one week of moving day and still not finished when we decide to call in a professional refinisher to put a stain and varnish on the bare wood. When he comes up to see the room, he looks around, runs his finger over the wood, and says not too gently, "Well, you know, of course, that this room is nowhere near ready to finish." We don't know. I am crushed. He picks up a corner block that has been stripped, but not cleaned, looks at it, and puts it down again in disgust. "This paint will never, never come out," he says. "All I'm trying to do is *salvage* this room. The woodwork is pine; it's soft. The fireplace is white oak. It will come out nicely, but the pine is too soft; we can *never* get the paint out." When I ask him what he plans to do, he says, "Oh, well, we have our tools, our tricks." When I try to get specific, like how he works with curves, he says, "We have our methods." He protects his arcane procedures, like some medieval alchemist, and he seems very arrogant, putting himself above the rest of us ordinary mortals.

So I stamp around muttering for a while, but we let him finish the room, and he later becomes a friend. The room looks beautiful. A Sherlock Holmes with a magnifying glass might find a few white streaks remaining, but the average viewer gets an impression of soft shining wood that almost seems to glow. The corner blocks are wonderful, their details now in high relief. Would we do it again? I don't know. We do decide on the basis of this experience that if the woodwork on the first floor is ever to be stripped, we will not be the ones to do it. And for right now, we are not making any plans to have it done. Maybe some time in the future. . . .

The third project we want to have finished before we move is the repair and refinishing of all the floors on the first two stories of the house. We have lived through floor refinishing before. We don't want to live through it again. The beautiful inlaid borders of the floors are damaged in some places. Pieces of the border are missing where radiator pipes went through. There are dark areas of water damage. Where the diagonal fireplace had been, the borders are nonexistent. A straight line marks the place where the fireplace stood, making an ugly scar in the beautiful floor. But who can do that kind of work? Our venerable floor man, reputed to be the best in the business, with three generations of floor people behind him, can do wonderful things with the bad modern patches, replacing them with old wood taken from the floors of closets; but even he cannot find anyone who can deal with the inlaid border. In one of our exploratory meetings with Susan, we mention the problem. She has an idea. A carpenter she knows is very good with woodworking. The holder of a bachelor's degree in fine arts, he is not likely to say, "We've never done it this way before, so we can't help you." He is more likely to say, "Someone did this somehow before; let's try to figure it out."

Harold Bend arrives with his compasses, planes, and miter box. He figures out that the inverted triangles in the pattern can be reversed, and soon he has glued together two strips of walnut separated by a strip of white oak which he then cuts in a zigzag pattern, making the inverted triangles. He saws tiny diamonds of birch, glues strips of walnut and white oak on the diagonal, and in a short time has made up about nine feet of border, which he uses to continue the border up to the present-day fireplace and to replace damaged spots in the living room and hall. Our excellent floor man does the rest, and the results are so beautiful and so rare that I behold those floors with wonder and ask myself for the hundredth time how anyone could have covered them with the cabbage rose carpet that appears in some of the early photographs.

With the floors, we are on our way. Fixing the floor seems to have shown us something, maybe that the possibilities can, indeed, become actualities. Without ever having made a conscious decision, we have fallen into restoration in much the way that two people who have been friends can suddenly discover that they have fallen in love. What was merely ordinary before now seems extraordinary. Nothing is changed; yet everything is changed. I feel imbued with a higher purpose, a dream. There is no turning back, I feel, even if the going does get rough.

About this time, Charlie and I sit down to assess our progress and to define policy. We did almost all the work on our old house ourselves, but having lived with plaster dust in one spot or another almost continuously for five years, and knowing that there is a limit to the length of time we can live in a constant mess, we decide at the outset that this time we will hire out most of the work — move along fast — get it finished on the exterior, anyway, in spite of the financial headache we know is coming. Besides, we do not know a soffit from a fascia board, and the thought of working from ladders forty to fifty feet high gives us sweaty palms.

We have interviewed several general contractors and decide to hire Susan Moore. In spite of her youthful appearance, she has demonstrated many times over the kind of knowledge and interest it takes to redo an old house like this. Besides, she was the only contractor who actually climbed up on the roof to examine the chimneys. The others just stood on the ground and pointed. We will work along with Susan, and with the people she hires, taking over certain areas as our own. At the beginning, Charlie's area is windows. He will make sure they all open and close, replacing cords and weights as needed, ordering new storms. My area is planning and coordinating. I see my job as being akin to that of a magazine editor, with the responsibility of keeping the magazine on course as well as defining that course. Susan is managing editor; the others are writers, layout people, graphic designers, marketing, and so forth.

But I am also an errand runner, a go-fer, and I fail in the first job I assign myself.

It is my task to find a piece of molding that will match the door and window casings throughout the house in order to have it duplicated for the kitchen. We discover a small piece, painted pink, supporting a shelf in our bedroom closet; armed with that, I set out thinking I am on an hour's errand to find a millwork shop to duplicate the pattern. Two days later, I am still looking for a shop that will do what I want. I have traversed the metropolitan area from one side to another, logging probably 150 miles, have talked to twenty people, looked at hundreds of samples of moldings. When I do finally make a connection with someone who can do the work, I neglect to get the order in writing, and though I am sure I requested half birch and half oak, I receive twice as much birch as we need and no oak. Trying again, I order oak, but don't specify which kind, white or red, not knowing there is a difference, and get the wrong kind. I am contrite. Charlie is generous. "A few hundred dollars slipping through the crack isn't much on a job like this," he says gently. "We'll be lucky if it's only three times that much." It isn't.

The "small cosmetic kitchen job" proves to be rather larger than we thought. When we remove the suspended ceiling in order to restore the ceiling to its original height, we find that all the electrical wires, encased in corrugated Greenfield pipe that looks like large silver worms, have been suspended too and will now need to be buried in the wall. Digging into the walls produces showers of plaster so great it is like being in the midst of an archaeological expedition. Large splotches of lath are exposed, and we end up taking down the kitchen cabinets, putting in new wallboard and nailing the cabinets up again. The new ceiling looks fresh and smooth, but when we try to put on the new wallpaper, the tendency of the border to disappear into the ceiling makes us realize that the ceiling has waves; indeed, it slopes, more than slightly, toward the front of the house. Harold, who did not do the kitchen work, blames a probable crack in one of the joists overhead. It should have been repaired when the ceiling was open. I reply that it's too late now, and besides, wavy floors and ceilings are part of the charm of an old house. They attest to the authenticity of its age, like wrinkles on an old person's face.

The kitchen floor, though, is smooth. But the new wood

flooring has been laid over the old, raising the floor by a minuscule amount, just enough so the dishwasher won't slide into
its slot next to the sink.

Two days before moving day, I come over to the new house
late in the afternoon, after everyone has left, and find water all
over the kitchen floor. I can't find where it is coming from. I try
the faucet on the kitchen sink; nothing comes out. Quickly,
then, I run to the downstairs bathroom. Nothing. Upstairs,
nothing. Third floor — still nothing. I charge back down. Under
the kitchen sink, I find the two copper pipes to the faucet have
been sawn off, the ends left hanging like severed arteries, and
out of the stumps of the pipes wells the water. Probably the
only two copper pipes in the house, and they're sawn off! The
only thing in the kitchen that worked, the sink, is totally dis-
abled. There is some maniac at work here! I call Charlie. I call
the electrician. Both are out. This is crazy. I zoom to the basement, looking for the water meter. Can't find it. Gas, yes, but,
of course, the water meter is in an obscure spot.

I trace the water pipes backward from the hot water heater,
find where they enter the house. There are two shutoff valves.
One is tightly shut. The other is not. I tighten the loose one.
The water stops. But the crazy person who has done this might
still be somewhere in the house. I don't dare leave, don't dare
stay, and certainly don't dare go exploring. So I sit huddled in
the darkening kitchen, and finally the phone rings. It is the
electrician, returning my call. "Water on the floor?" he asks.
"Oh dear, how could that be? I *know* I turned off the water
when I sawed the pipes."

"You sawed off the pipes? Perfectly good pipes?" I scream.
"The only visible copper pipes in this house, and you *sawed
them off*? How could you saw off perfectly good pipes that work?

We're moving in two days, and you make our kitchen sink inoperable. How could you?"

"But Susan told me to," he replies. "She said we were going to move the whole sink cabinet to get it up high enough to put the dishwasher under it."

"We didn't decide any such thing," I angrily retort, ready to slam down the phone. But as he continues explaining, I calm down. He did shut off the water intake valve in the basement, but he hadn't realized there were two. Together we remember that the painter had been working in the basement. He had been using water in the basement sink, and when he left, shutting the tap, it had created enough pressure to cause the water to bubble up into the kitchen. Susan could not reach me. She talked to Charlie, and he gave her the go-ahead to move the cabinet. In the end, we do not move the cabinet. The wallpaper is already on, the floor sealers are coming the next day, a small slot in the overhang of the counter takes care of the dishwasher problem; but the episode is a lesson for me. Or rather, it is an indoctrination. I will realize, later, that small miscommunications such as this are commonplace, and that I'd better change my outlook if I am going to roll with the waves — I can't afford to be swamped each time there is a mishap.

# II

# BLACK LENSES

## April 4–Moving Day

I hear a sickening crunch when I try to close the first box I pack. Sure enough, three of our very best dinner plates lie broken on the bottom, crushed by inexperience and a cast iron frying pan.

We are moving ourselves, like gypsies. A ratty old wooden trailer, with spoked wheels taken from a 1920s automobile and a neighbor's junk pile, is our chief conveyance; our own backs (with some help), our labor. That we have only three blocks to go is a godsend, because we load that trailer time and time again with yards and yards of steel pipe, long wide yellow extension cords, piles of old moldings and door casings that Charlie has collected over the years, extraneous bits of lumber, saws, drills, fifteen kinds of nails and screws (totaling twenty-four thousand), and cans and cans of paint, thinking they might come in handy in our restoration. Little by little, load after load, like squirrels bringing nuts to their winter pantry, we fill up our basement, and now, no one can walk in it.

## April 5

We moved in our last box at 6:15 this evening. Tonight is our first in the new house. We climb exhausted into bed, turn out the light, and are just settling in when the chandelier in the little sitting room off our bedroom falls to the floor, smashing some of its light bulbs and creating a huge gouge in the newly finished floor. An inauspicious omen? I shudder uncomfortably, then remember that on the day we took possession of our last house, we opened the door to the third-floor stairs and found a dead bat, which I worried about for months; and yet we spent eleven very happy years in that house. Maybe seemingly inauspicious omens are auspicious for us.

## April 6

Work begins in earnest today. Susan had told us that a scaffold would be arriving today, Monday, but with the moving and all, I haven't thought much about it — what it will be used for, who will work on it. Besides, it is the first day of school after spring vacation, and around 8:00 in the morning, I am trying to get the children off to school — find their book bags, jackets, and mittens, all of which seem to have been lost, put away in God knows which one of dozens of boxes — when a large truck arrives with the scaffold. This is not a little scaffold, made out of a few planks that hang by ropes from the roof, but a huge freestanding structure that reaches up three stories, and it is all in pieces of steel pipe. A few minutes later, a ton of lumber arrives in the alley on a big flatbed truck. Delivery men ask me where to put things. I have no idea.

The children go to school without jackets, and our six-month-old puppy escapes and runs down to the lake. I chase after her, my red bathrobe billowing out behind me, and am soon joined by a few young men who have arrived to work on the house. We fly up and down the lake shore in pursuit, looking like adherents of one of the more bizarre religious sects that come to the lake to practice their rituals. Eventually one of the young men tackles her and comes bearing her up the front steps like Jesus with his lamb. This is our introduction to Frank, one of the four carpenters who will be our daily companions for the next three months. Frank is about six feet four inches tall, weighs perhaps 220 pounds, is broad in the shoulders, and has a shock of blond hair that he is forever tossing out of his eyes. He is a sculptor by profession, and he has already told me that he will eventually go back to his native Germany with his wife to await the birth of their child, so that the baby will have both German and American citizenship. Less exotic, but no less interesting, are the two other dogcatchers, both carpenters. Art, whom we have met before, is a bluegrass-blues banjo player and a friend of Harold, the floor genius. Art is full of energy and very voluble. He hopes to go to medical school in the fall and is married to an attorney who works for the Legal Aid Society. Finally, more quiet and soft spoken, Paul is a slightly built, bearded man, whose shy smile promises a gentle nature.

At lunch time, taking a break from moving boxes and trying to decide which to unpack next, I come into the kitchen and find eight people jammed around the table: the four carpenters, including Harold, who is to be in charge of the others; two electricians, who are finishing the work on the kitchen; Susan Moore; and Susan's six-month-old baby daughter, Molly. Molly is cooing away at Aggie, this morning's escapee, a golden retriever, who is getting very excited about all these people and their lunch boxes. I am excited — elated, even — feeling that we are at the start of high adventure; and I am happy as I start unpacking some of the boxes we have brought with us. Unpacking, that is, in a somewhat haphazard fashion. I want only essential items, and I have to rummage for them. It is not long before half-unpacked boxes and their contents are strewn all over the house. I have created minor chaos, unlike Kate, who has managed to make some order in her nest. She went right to work the moment she arrived. The first thing she did was to line up her small stuffed animals on a shelf above the fireplace, and her small china creatures on her desk. She put all her hardcover books in one bookcase, all the paperbacks in another, piled her games neatly in the closet, folded the shirts in her drawers. She was unpacked before the rest of us had opened a suitcase. Thank heavens we got her room ready first! Chris doesn't seem to mind wading around in tangles of model railroad tracks, and Charlie and I just shut our eyes to the mess.

### April 14

A large orange dumpster arrives and is parked out in front of the house. Two of the carpenters begin ripping off the outer skin of the house — the big, square, "new" shakes that have been covering up the Victorian shingles for at least forty years.

We start with the shingles because, frankly, we can't wait to see what is underneath. Removing the shingles first does not alter Susan's plan of working from the roof down, however. Before the new roof can go on, all the rotten wood in the soffits and roof supports has to be replaced, and while two of the carpenters begin to work in that area, the other two are ripping off shingles so that we can get rid of what is rotten there, too.

We begin with the shakes that have been covering the large half-moon stained glass window on the stairs. Everyone is curious about that. It takes half a day to remove what has been there for forty years. The light pours through, and it is wonderful, glorious! The colors are deep and rich — purples and greens, mostly, with strands of ocher and flowers of soft turquoise with patterns of ribbons and leaves surrounding a central medallion. In the morning, the purples are the dominant color; in the afternoon, with the western sun, the window takes on a rosy cast. It is apparent, though, that the window will have to be repaired. There are cracks of light between some of the pieces of glass and the lead that binds them. The window is badly buckled. Harold crawls up on the ledge to test the window's solidity. It feels strong. None of the pieces of glass is wiggling. He thinks the carpenters can work around the window and remove it later when it is more convenient.

The next day, we start on the front of the house. The shingles come off quickly, fly through the air, pile up on the ground and in the dumpster. Passersby wander right up on the front lawn to ask what is happening. Who ever heard of peeling a house as one would an orange? The front of the house is peeled over a period of five days. The shingles underneath are light brown, contrasting nicely with the white trim, which we can really see for the first time standing out against this darker background. The personality of the house is revealed to be delightful, light and graceful, not a white elephant at all.

Saturday night it rains. The next day, Easter, we are wakened at 5:30 A.M. by a noise that goes plunk, splat, splat. Big drops of water are coming out of the twenty-foot ceiling in the hall and falling on the stairs below. We run for the buckets — a dishpan, ice cream containers, two cast-off diaper pails — even-

tually assembling seven, which stand like a group of motley
sentinels guarding the stairs, forcing us to wend our way
around them. I am concerned about the leaks, but no one else
seems particularly worried. The rain stops around noon, and
we have a lovely Easter, with fifteen relatives coming back here
after lunch to view our new folly. We have a party, in fact, for
it is a beautiful Easter; there is a real parade going around the
lake. Neighbors, friends, hundreds of people from the city and
the suburbs are out for a stroll, taking advantage of the delightful weather to walk around the lake. As we spot friends in the
crowd, we wave and call them over. Soon we have quite a
gathering and are kept busy sending out for beer and pizza.
The water in the stairwell keeps dripping, ominously and per-
versely, I think, in the face of all this sunshine. It continues for
more than eight hours after the rain stops, not letting up until
9:00 at night.

## April 20

Monday morning the carpenters begin with the north side of
the house. The roof is sagging badly there. This area of sagging
roof extends out over the balconies off Kate's and our rooms, as
well as over part of Chris's room. We have to jack the balconies
up and reinforce them before the new roof goes on, since ulti-
mately, they are what holds up the roof. If the balconies sag,
they pull the roof with them. Our first task is to rebuild the
balcony outside Kate's room and make new curved supports
underneath.

A band saw roars outside Kate's window, blanketing the yard
with corkscrew shavings that look like fleece. A large stack of
lumber leans against the house. (At least now I know where I

should have told the delivery men to put it that first day. We had to move it ourselves from the alley.) To make the curved supports for the porch, the carpenters do a curious thing. They saw small cuts into one side of the wood, spacing them every half inch or so, and then bend the board. I had thought they would have to soak thinner strips of wood and laminate them, as with skis, but evidently not. Harold says he will use the laminating process, though, for the balcony railings.

Monday afternoon I do the laundry for the first time. I am even looking forward to that usually onerous task, because we have chosen to use the small bedroom off the bathroom on the second floor for our laundry, instead of a cold, unheated basement room. I feel very fortunate to have such a "utility room" and imagine, falsely, that I will wear freshly ironed shirts all summer. The second load of wash drains all over the floor. Gallons and gallons of dirty, soapy water pour out and spread slowly all over the recently refinished floor. Worse still, the water runs through the brand-new Sheetrock kitchen ceiling below and drips in a steady stream onto the kitchen floor. We are going to lose that ceiling, and it was put in just two weeks ago. I am distraught and call Charlie, burst into tears before I can tell him what is wrong. The electrician who installed the washing machine failed to attach the drain hose securely to the drainpipe — he just stuck the hose in the pipe, even though it is written in red ink and in capital letters and *underlined* on the instructions that the hose will jump out of the drainpipe if it is not held by a wire. Susan asks Harold to drill holes in the kitchen ceiling to release the water. Maybe we will lose only part of the ceiling.

I leave for an appointment and come home at 5:30 to find half of the turquoise central medallion in the big stained glass window lying on the stair carpet. The window will have to be removed right away. It is too fragile to withstand the vibrations from the ladders and hammers. I am upset about the window, and I am upset about the electrician's carelessness. We are going to have to let him go — fire him — and he was a friend, even if he did make a few careless mistakes, like dropping the refrigerator on the floor and drilling a hole through the dining room floor in our previous house. In this one, he has been unable to complete the wiring job promised a month and a half ago. The washing machine is just the last in a series of mishaps. Charlie agrees to do the dirty work, but both of us are sad and frustrated. When Kate comes bounding down the stairs, her usual energy roiling around her like dust around a stagecoach, she slips on a piece of plastic covering the stairs and knocks over two of the water-filled buckets, creating a mess of plastic sheeting, plaster, and water. I yell at her, accuse her of never looking where she is going, and order her peremptorily to the third floor to watch TV. It has not been the best of days.

### *April 21*

Tuesday morning, Harold starts to remove the half-moon window. It rains again. The plunks and splats on the stairs recur, much worse this time, faster and harder. Paint and plaster in the leaking ceiling slowly fold back and drop, falling two stories down the open stairwell. I am terrified that this whole five-hundred-pound ceiling will crash to the floor. It is eroding fast, and soon will slide away in great chunks like an avalanche.

But we have learned something. I remember how Harold released the water from the kitchen ceiling. We get a step ladder, poke holes in the soggy part of the ceiling with the biggest screwdriver we can find. Nothing much happens at first, but finally, after jabbing frantically at the ceiling, brave knights with tiny lances, we push through the Sheetrock and old plaster, and twenty pounds of water cascade down, almost overflowing the giant diaper pail I am currently using as our main leak catcher. We hold it steady so the force of the water will not knock it down.

## April 30

Susan originally hoped that we could use as much as 80 percent of the old shingles. Now it appears that well over 50 percent are rotten, and so is all the trim — including dentil moldings shaped like rows of squat jack-o'-lantern teeth, curved and doubled fascia boards outlining the eaves, and door and window casings — all together running into the thousands of linear board feet. Harold discovers that an army of big, black, shiny carpenter ants, which love the moist, rotten wood, have been at work all over the balconies, tunneling their way in and around so many of the railings that we will have to replace every last one. Breathing deeply, we revise our estimates upward. Boxes and boxes of new fish-scale shingles arrive from the lumberyard. We are lucky restoration fever has caught hold in so much of the country and that Minneapolis, in contrast to its slightly older sister, Saint Paul, is one of the last places to succumb. A whole industry is spotted across the country engaged in making all sorts of products that were unavailable ten years ago, and we can order the thousands of shingles we will need, instead of cutting them by hand, as in the old days. In Minneapolis we can also find original materials in the antique shops and salvage places, which have not been scoured and picked over as they have in other areas of the country where restoration has been popular for some time.

Susan thinks it will be easier to paint the shingles with primer *before* they are put on the house, so one fine spring day, Marty, the painter, lays 580 shingles out flat on pieces of plastic that placed end to end would cover half a football field. He sprays the shingles with paint, then leaves them to dry for several hours. Unfortunately a twenty-five-mile-an-hour wind comes up, and the shingles begin to blow all over. They fly and spin like maple-seed helicopters, but are much more dangerous — small boomerangs. They stick in the trees, roll across the boulevard into the park. Marty and I spend the afternoon scurrying after the rolling, flapping shingles. It reminds me of the time I had to chase after tumbling headless chickens on a farm and gather them up in bags for plucking. I never knew which way they would go; I'd be running in one direction, and then suddenly, they would turn and appear to chase me, as if they were still alive — or worse, were possessed by diabolical spirits.

### May 10

This spring is very wet and rainy, and it seems to rain inside the house as much as it does outside. Fixing the source of our leaks has become a high priority, but finding this elusive source is proving to be difficult. Water can enter almost anywhere and travel along sloping beams. Where it emerges as a leak in the ceiling can be tens of feet from where it enters the house. With Susan's help, we consider as sources the roof over our little sitting room and the wall above the south deck, and we cover them with plastic sheeting — but to no avail. The water continues to come through. Now we think leaks in the floor of the south metal deck, which is directly above the stairwell, are responsible. Tar pots still repose outside the door to the deck, and globules of the black sticky stuff are abundant all over its metal surface, attesting to many repairs and attempts at repair over the years. We know further patching will be self-defeating. The whole deck will have to come off, be rebuilt so that it slopes away rather than toward the house, and then be redecked with metal at the same time the roofers finish with the main roof, since they, not the carpenters, deal with metal sheeting.

## *May 11*

The carpenters go to work; they remove one metal roof, then another, and another and another and on and on. Evidently previous owners' solutions to leaks in the stairwell ceiling were simply to slap a new metal roof over the old one just beneath. When the carpenters finish, they have removed *eight* metal roofs, stacked one on top of another, and the back yard immediately below the deck looks like a junk yard where the trash masher has gone berserk.

While the carpenters are working on the deck, the chimney man is busy tearing down and rebuilding two huge Victorian chimneys, and I am rapidly learning a whole new vocabulary. "Corbel" is not just a kind of champagne, but a kind of outcropping or projection; around the corbel at the top of our chimney march "soldiers," so named only if the bricks stand upright, vertical. If the bricks lie down, in a horizontal position, they can no longer be called soldiers, but are, instead, demoted to mere "courses." I also learn, during this period, that I should be glad, rather than alarmed, when the day comes to "break" the gutters. The term means "put them on the house," not "chop them apart."

Mr. Johnson, the chimney man, is a conscientious, long-time brickworker, about sixty years old. He is the only one of our workers who belongs to a union, and a building trades strike threatens to be called next Wednesday, only five days away. This proposed strike makes us very nervous indeed, because until the chimneys are finished, the roof can't go on, and until the roof is on, the house will continue to get damper and damper. We have been urging Mr. Johnson to hurry, please!

Today, Friday, the weather is lovely, warm and sunny for once. Mr. Johnson works all day taking apart the crumbling old chimney on the west gable, the chimney containing the flue for the furnace. In the evening, we entertain some of our first guests. We are sitting in the living room when one of them comes in from the kitchen saying she can smell gas. Running to the kitchen, we approach the stove, and our eyes fill with water and our noses begin to burn, but we can't smell gas coming from the stove. We open the basement door and get halfway down the stairs. The air is much worse there, so bad we can't breathe, acrid and painful. We can barely make out the shape of a bare light bulb glowing weakly, suspended in the haze. We turn and run back up the stairs.

"We have to do something," I scream. "Charlie, call someone! Call the fire department! Call the gas company! Call Minnegasco!"

"Don't panic!" says my husband, calm as always. "Take it easy."

I am convinced that his olfactory nerves have gone dead. He doesn't realize the urgency of the situation.

"I'm not panicking," I answer, my voice rising to the hysterical pitch that is beginning to be my second nature. "I'm not panicking at all; I'm just going to wake up the children and get them out of their beds and take them over to your mother's before they're asphyxiated. Please call the gas company!"

I am terrified, sure that the house is on fire.

I start to run out of the room, but Charlie grabs my arm. He asks what has been different about today, what the men have been working on.

"The west chimney," I manage to stammer.

Of course. There is our answer. Part of the crumbling chimney has fallen into the flue, blocking it. No one realized this during the day because it has been too warm for the furnace to go on, but now, when the night is cold. . . . So we call Mr. Johnson, who feels very bad, but confirms our hypothesis. He thinks he removed all the debris, but maybe some got through. We shut off the furnace, put a screen over the opening to keep out bats, and spend a cool night. If the furnace had gone on even an hour later, we would all have been asleep and might never have awakened.

It has been frightening, this little experience, and it brings into my consciousness some painful things that I have been trying very hard not to see. And deal with. Some basic concepts, and what they mean to me. Like a roof over one's head. A home. Security. And what happens when, for a while, one feels, emotionally speaking, as if one has no home? And what of those poor souls who have, literally, no home at all?

Some of my underpinnings have been removed. Between the beginning of packing up to move and the bulk of unpacking, maybe three weeks later, I felt — homeless. I became irrationally angry when I drove by our former house and saw the new owner's car in "our" driveway, up against the gate that Charlie

had built there. I missed the neighbors, their smiles, our chats
— but that happens with every move. This one has a further
turn of the screw, because in this case, the roof is literally caving
in. For a while, I have a sense that the whole experience of
buying this old house and fixing it up is an adventure, something to write home about, like a college student's summer
backpacking trip. A little risk, a little test. If things don't work
out, you can always turn around and go back. You *can* go home
again.

But in our case, there is, of course, no safe secure home to go
back to. Making a new beginning means making a break. We
have cut the rope, set ourselves adrift; or rather *I* have. In our
marriage, the home has been my main arena, the center ring in
the three-ring circus that is our lives, and now I have the feeling
that I have wrecked our home, wrecked all its systems, and not
yet set up any replacements. This move, this restoration, this
mess we are in is something major that *I* have pushed for, and
for which I am, therefore, largely responsible; not something
that my husband has chosen, which has been the case with
previous moves. I feel responsible for everyone's happiness and
unhappiness, though reason tells me I am not. On bad days,
when the children or Charlie is unhappy because of something
going on with the house, I feel I am tossing my family over-
board and am kicking the lifeboat away: Swim, everyone, and
smile while you do it, dammit. *Please!*

I had thought we were prepared for a little chaos. As newlyweds we had lived in France for three years, fifty miles and
two hundred years from Paris. We coped with a suitcase-size
coal furnace in an outdoor cellar that we had to feed with shov-
els of coal twice a day. No thermostat, either, just a door we set
to a certain level to control the draft. Long underwear, wool

slacks, turtlenecks and sweaters, fingerless gloves, gas water heaters that either went out leaking gas or exploded. No frozen orange juice, frozen pizza, frozen vegetables — no freezer at all, for that matter. And we didn't miss them a bit. Granted, my greatest wish upon returning to the U.S. was warmth; but in the intervening ten years, with energy an issue, I once again grew inured to a six-month uniform of long underwear and sweater.

Besides, living in France taught me that there was more than one way to skin a cat — people's digestive systems will continue to work whether they have their roast chicken at noon or at night. French babies will grow up just as well as American ones, even if they don't have any orange juice before six months of age. It is not written in stone that things have to be done in certain immutable ways. Often no particular way is best, only different. I was prepared, I had thought; but I wasn't. For one thing, I forgot that in France we had had no children. I hadn't realized how much our house, our home, was a refuge, a place of relative order amid the chaos, the hurly-burly, the car-pools, the schedules. It was there; it worked; it demanded no adjustments from me. I didn't have to adapt.

What is difficult about living with a restoration, or any kind of major remodeling, is that there *is* no island of tranquillity to which one can escape, except maybe the public library. If things go wrong at the work place, one can go home. If things go wrong at home, there is the office. Each may have its problems, but there is a change of venue. In a restoration, the home becomes another work place. When a pipe bursts, for example, the result may be not only a fight with the spouse whose policies caused the break, but also the cleanup, the rotten soggy stink, the washing machine loads of sodden, mildewing rags, and sometimes, the emotional aftershock. There is no cool, finished room to which to retreat for a few hours to regroup. Everywhere are peeling wallpaper, missing corner blocks, exposed plaster, hanging window stops, open toolboxes — no place that expresses that sense of inner peace and serenity we think of as our home, be it only a room. In a restoration, everything is temporary. One lives out of boxes; nothing is put back or placed where it ought to go, including dishes and glasses, mittens and hats and scarves, furniture; and it changes every day. No one can find anything. There is a continuous sense of chaos.

It has taken a while for my feeling of homelessness to subside. I have had to admit into my consciousness the grief I felt over the loss of our old home, to imagine in detail the little room where I nursed our babies, the brass hardware that Charlie so lovingly polished, the beveled glass that we treasured. But that part of our lives is over. I have finally packed my emotional suitcases too. I wonder if some of the women who crossed the country in Conestoga wagons ever felt this way. Initial enthusiasm for a great adventure, followed by a sudden sense of being bereft, of having no place to rest, to put their feet down, of thinking, My God, what have I done? Or did they always follow their men, never initiating the journey themselves? And is this *why* I felt so bereft? Because men have done it for thousands of years, uprooted their families and plunked them down again in a strange spot. *They* were not crushed by feelings of responsibility for the unhappiness of their wives and children at their uprooting. They were *supposed* to have the dreams — of the new land, of the new life. It was up to the women to make the dreams come true — to follow along, bringing civilization in tow, starting the schools, teaching the ways of the people; for it was women, in the nineteenth century, who were the guardians of personal morality. Selfless, always concerned for others, they ensured the future by molding the next generation. Is it because I am going against these unspoken traditions without being able to let go of them that I am feeling so responsible when chaos descends and things fall apart?

Today, for instance, Susan and the roofing contractor come over to discuss roofs. Evidently the kind of roof we want, something called a Timberline, which closely resembles the old cedar shakes but costs half as much, isn't available right now. We will have to use something else, or wait. The roofing company has a similar roof we can put on right away. We sit in the kitchen, mulling this over. There is talk of hips and shoulders and flashing. I don't quite get it. It sounds vaguely sexual. My attention is focused on Chris, who is lying on the bare floor a short distance away curled up into a ball of misery. He has lost a toy car, ordinarily not a big thing.

Chris has a collection of special toy cars and trucks that have rubber tires, which for some reason he likes to remove. He keeps these tiny tires in a special box, and he is sure he put both the box and a red oil truck Charlie brought him from England on the hall table; and I'm sure he did too. Chris is the only one in the house who always remembers just where he puts things. But the hall table isn't in the hall anymore. The carpenters moved it when they set up a scaffold to work on the stairwell ceiling, and the car and box are gone. Chris had just come in from playing outside when he made that discovery. "I'll be up in a minute," I call when he yells out the news. But the minute stretches into five as the phone rings and Susan and the roofer arrive with samples of shingles. By the time I get upstairs, Chris is in a state, crying, throwing things, insisting over and over again on his red truck. Nothing else will do. Dissuading him is hopeless. He also needs lunch. He follows me into the kitchen, all the time wailing, and occasionally flailing at me.

He lies on the kitchen floor, wailing his refrain in front of Susan and the roofer and all the carpenters who are sitting around the kitchen table, and I slap together a peanut butter and jelly sandwich as fast as I can, stepping over him as I move from counter to cupboard and back again. I reach down to try to pick him up, but he elbows me away. One of the carpenters tries to intercede, telling Chris that "big boys don't cry," and offering to help him build a road with another toy.

But Chris just curls up into a little ball, shriveled, defeated. The carpenters finish their lunch and go out. I start my discussion with Susan and the roofer.

So Chris lost a toy car. An ordinary, everyday occurrence with small boys, nothing to get worked up about. That's what I keep telling myself. But the truth is, I'm worried. Chris would not have acted like this two months ago.

## May 25

The roofers have been here for nearly a week now, ripping off the old roof, adding great piles of black asphalt shingles to the rubble massed below the south deck. I wonder if any remnant of my buried, trampled peonies will survive to flourish again next year when the mess is over. We seem to have hit a lucky streak, no rain this week, though we are prepared with rolls of heavy-duty polyethylene just in case. Mr. Johnson *did* finish the chimneys in the nick of time, just hours before the strike was called.

The carpenters have been putting the railings on the south deck, trying to get them finished before the sheet-metal roofers come to lay on the skin that we hope will be totally impermeable — no more leaks! The carpenters are a little behind in their work, and the sheet-metal roofers arrive before Harold and the others are finished. One of the roofers, the young son of the owner of the business, barely out of his teens, gets into a disagreement with Harold over who will have possession of the south deck for the next few days. There is not enough room for both of them to work at once. Harold has a relaxed and confident personality that can tolerate all kinds of intrusions and interruptions — a delivery that isn't made or that is erroneously filled, a coworker's impatience, personality conflicts. He reminds me a little of Jean-Paul Belmondo in looks and temperament — lots of energy — yet his is a soothing personality. He may have a disagreement with Susan over how to proceed, but he states his case forthrightly and calmly and does not get into a fight.

So it is with great surprise that I hear Harold shouting, "You dumb jerk!" and later, "Stupid young punk, doesn't know anything, just likes to throw his weight around." The roofer's son is insisting that Harold vacate the deck before the railings are finished; but the sheet metal has to cover the base of the railings, so of course the railings have to be finished first — all of which Harold has pointed out at great length. Harold threatens to take our business elsewhere. The roofer threatens to quit. But eventually the roofer yields to Harold's superior logic and agrees to work on something else first. Susan lets Harold know that such delays must not be repeated. I am not convinced that the roofer is so terribly arrogant; he has shown me some consideration by urging me to call him any time, "even at 5:00 A.M.," if there is the slightest problem, the tiniest bit of moisture. So I don't think he is too bad. But then, I don't have to take sides. I can watch from the benches. Disputes of this type are Susan's problem, not mine. For once.

In spite of the dispute, the south deck is a pleasant place to be this week. There is a constant hum of activity, rather like a beehive; but bees have the edge as far as organization is concerned. Yesterday one of the carpenters, a bird watcher by avocation, spotted a rare Tennessee warbler from this airy balcony, and the whole crew stopped work while I fetched the binoculars and Peterson's guide for an impromptu meeting of the Audubon Society. Another carpenter is a fan of Garrison Keillor's writing, and I was enjoying his stimulating analyses and reviews until I suddenly remembered that these enjoyable conversations were costing exorbitant amounts of money, and I would do well to keep my mouth shut — or confine my comments to pleasantries about the weather, when there is weather to be pleasant about.

## May 26

The new ceiling over the stairwell is nearly finished. Art is doing the final taping today. Tomorrow he will sand for the last time, and then, down comes the scaffold, away go the drop cloths, and we can stop sliding down the stairs. No more water spots, no more falling plaster, no more feeling as if the roof is caving in over our heads. I feel as if a burden has been lifted off my shoulders, now that there is a good tight ceiling, and I chat happily with Art as he slaps on the last of the plasterlike "mud" with his trowel. We are talking about his wife, an attorney who, Art says, has been working so hard, twelve hours a day, that she thinks she is developing an ulcer. She is not yet thirty.

"Can't she slow down a bit? Work less, maybe part time?" I ask.

"No," Art replies. "She is too committed. She feels such a part of the women's movement, fighting for the opportunity to achieve. To slow down would be like letting down the troops."

I ponder this as I go about my work, this sense of linkage strong enough to command such a sacrifice. Such a wall of solidarity. The individual gets lost. Is Art's wife in some way holding on to the old traditions too? Do her feelings of betrayal stem from that very core of feeling responsible for other people?

I am startled out of these ruminations by a crash, followed by an "Oh shit." Art has dropped the trowel, which has delivered a glancing blow and a new dent to the banister. It doesn't bother me. We have been talking about stripping the banister, which would mean repairing the dent in the process. On the other hand, I wouldn't mind leaving the dent there. Its edges would grow softer little by little as years of fingers and dust cloths, and now and then a new coat of paint, make it almost disappear. In time only the fingers of an expert, like Susan's when she discovered the depression on the mantel, would be able to tell that there ever was an accident. I don't mind the dent. We have just added one of our own to those of the past hundred years.

## May 29

Now that the south deck is finished, the carpenters go to work on the back of the house, replacing the rotten old paneling with new wood. We find some metal numbers marking our address, probably put there during the 1930s. We will save them and put them on the garage later.

Aggie, the puppy, is driving us to distraction. She runs off with the carpenters' tools and hats and gloves constantly, and we have to drop everything to chase her, and of course she loves it. Unfortunately, we are reverse conditioning her, giving her a dog biscuit each time she relinquishes some object, so she has been getting worse and worse, taking more and more things. The loss of my best sweater was the last straw — she *ate* the stag-horn buttons. That the buttons were made of bone is *not* enough to consider an extenuating circumstance. The fact is, she jumped up and snatched the sweater from the kitchen counter, and now there are seven gaping holes where the buttons used to be. It's the basement for her, this time, for sure!

The weather is nice, though, and nothing bothers us too much. Today, for instance, is warm and sunny, a day to appreciate the apple blossoms that mound the trees by the lake. As we work outside, enjoying the air, we notice a woman wandering around the front yard. Rather pretty, appearing to be in her late thirties, she seems very curious, more than just a gawker. Investigating, we learn that she is the daugher of the Kelly family who lived in the house from 1945 until the 1960s. She is meeting her three sisters for a birthday picnic down by the lake — they have been drawn by all the activity on their old stomping ground. As they all arrive, we invite them in for a tour. They have not returned since they left the house, and as their mother was very ill and they lost their father while living here, their reacquaintance is an emotional homecoming for them, as well as an unexpected source of information for us, not unlike the sudden discovery of a trunk full of old letters in the attic.

We learn about the leaks that have been coming through the stairwell ceiling since at least 1945 and their father's annual trek to the south deck with his tar pot. It was one of the sisters who was responsible for some odd-looking dents we discovered in

Kate's door, and it was their mother who put up the pink closet wallpaper that resembles the spun sugar candy tulle formals I wore in the 1950s. It was she, also, who tore down the front porch and installed the white filigreed iron railing that borders the terrace and frames the front door. She removed the oak paneling beneath the staircase, too. The hall was too dark, she felt; the paneling and the porch made it darker; besides, the porch was rotten. The piano had stood where our sofa now sat, and vice versa; one of the large mirrors in the living room had been placed to reflect the lake; the large mirror in the dining room had, indeed, been designed to cover up the "ugly" stained glass window. Their parents, too, had put the white square shingles over the Victorian fish scales on the second floor and had covered over the half-moon stained glass window on the stairway. It was all part of a "remodeling" in the 1950s, an attempt to make the house look more modern.

We learn where there had been parties, and laughter, where there had been tears, and once again the house becomes alive in another time frame, peopled by the ghosts of the past. I wonder what other ghosts we will discover. I'm sure that somewhere in the house there is a secret compartment. Someday we will find it.

## June 1

Although this is a good time, still my fuse is short, simply because of the phone calls, mess, noises, and lack of privacy, which goes with having so many people around all the time (our belief that working on the outside of the house would mean that the interior would be free from disruption has proved to be pure fiction). Today a dear old friend of mine offers to do some cleaning for us. This woman helped raise me and my brother and sister, and now advises and nurtures us like a beloved aunt. I am away from the house all day, and when I come in, she starts complaining about soot in the upstairs fireplace, where Susan has been poking around, trying to find a way to make an unused flue operational again.

"The soot is everywhere," she says accusingly. "Why can't they stop this? Why can't they be neater? It's not worth my cleaning, that's all."

I have worked all day at a convention with lots of people and am already feeling very harassed, and I explode. "They're going to keep doing it, making these messes. We're constructing. I didn't know you were going to wash woodwork. Don't try to do those big things, for heaven's sake! Just vacuum and dust. We have to live here, you know."

She bursts into tears. I feel guilty, unable to sympathize.

Later that evening, Aggie escapes the confines of the kitchen and runs upstairs and jumps on our king-size bed. Throwing myself across the bed, I try to tackle her as she dodges this way and that, barking at me, but I can't reach her. In a fury, I grab a pillow and start swinging at her. The pillow snags on her tooth, ripping open. As the air above the bed fills with feathers, Aggie leaps about, snapping at them, trying to eat them. She looks and acts rabid, with feathers stuck all over her mouth, like foam. Rabid is just how I feel.

*June 2*

I am revising my own private job description — through evolution, not revolution. Charlie and Susan are taking over as editors. I am bumping myself upstairs to publisher and demoting myself firmly, this time, to go-fer. I just don't know enough about construction to make all the daily decisions, and I made a few bad ones, such as allowing Mr. Johnson to use some of the old bricks on the back chimney. We now have a jagged line traversing the chimney, dividing it into sections of light and dark red, and it doesn't look very good.

I still make some of the minor decisions, of course, like whether to spend eighty or two hundred dollars on a plywood floor that doesn't show; but in most cases, I consult with Charlie, or leave the details to him entirely. We both thought at first that my taking the burden of the decision making would relieve him of the responsibility and free him up a bit, but details of construction are more his province than mine. He knows more about them, and he *cares* more about them. This shifting of responsibility works better and is a relief to me, since I can get very opinionated and rigid when I have staked out a claim to an area in which I have little knowledge — like making an "opening three" bid in bridge, a shutout, showing little strength. I am much more flexible in areas where I know more, which is, I suppose, the generosity of security.

## June 6

We have more meetings with Susan, get more figures, approach the problems of windows and the porch. The windows are in terrible shape. The frame of almost every storm window is rotten; in many cases the glass is hanging free. We will need new storms on *all* the windows. We consider combination storms and screens, made of either wood or vinyl, but they are unsatisfactory because this house was designed to be cooled by convection currents, meaning that the very tall windows will have to open at the top as well as at the bottom. In most of our interior windows, the check rail (the place where the top and bottom "halves" of the window meet) is two-thirds of the way up. We cannot find top and bottom openings in combination windows with check rails at that height, and if the interior and exterior windows do not match at this dividing point, looking through them will be like looking through slats. We opt to go the old way, using conventional storms and screens in most of the windows, a feasible alternative only because every bedroom has its own balcony, making handling the seventy-five-pound storm windows relatively easy. There are only four windows that will have to be hauled up and down ladders. Some of the windows are stationary, like the stained glass and the big plate glass windows in the front and side bays. For these we will have thermal-glass, or double-paned, storms permanently installed. On the turret, the storm windows are curved, and the cost of replacing them is so high that we postpone that decision, hoping to find some other solution.

Some of the interior sash is also rotten and will have to be replaced — just how much is being revealed to us slowly, as Charlie painstakingly works over every window in the house at the rate of one window per weekend day. *All* the windows have been painted shut, and not with just one easy-to-break coat of paint, but with at least four. We couldn't open a single window in the house when we moved in. Maybe that was why it was so cozy and warm in January, says a small voice in the back of my mind — but I choose not to pay attention just now. As Charlie releases a window from its bonds of paint and replaces the old sash cord, he pushes a knife into the wood surrounding the glass. Sometimes the wood is solid. Too often, the knife just sinks in with little or no resistance, and the whole window has to come out for replacement.

## *June 10*

Charlie has discovered Sam, a recent Soviet émigré and a whiz at making windows, working at our neighborhood hardware store. Together they work out a solution for the curved windows on the turret, no mean feat considering that Sam speaks almost no English, and Charlie no Russian. They find an intermediary in Barney, the owner of the store, who communicates with Sam in German, making theirs truly an international undertaking. Charlie saws pieces of wood in curves, trying to match the top and bottom check rails of the existing rotten storm windows. I carry the pieces of wood to Sam, who checks them to see if the bend in the wood matches the angle at which he has to install the glass. He most often looks at them, waves his hands crosswise, as if he is wiping out the dust of the world (or seven more hours of sawing, measuring, and calculating), and says, "No good. Iss no good."

I take the pieces of wood home, and Charlie tries again. And again. We celebrate with champagne the night Sam finally gives us thumbs up, his mark of highest approbation.

"Iss O.K." he says, and we are off and running, knowing we can relax, having received an accolade from a true craftsman.

Besides windows, our meetings with Susan concern the front porch. This large open area, the background for the 1894 lemonade pourers, is what was replaced by the filigreed-railing attempt at an arbor and the Greek-type pediment in the 1950s. Our question: should we go ahead and restore the porch, or should we just leave the front terrace as it is? The cost is considerable, for both the carpentry work and the stone. The value of the porch is almost entirely aesthetic, its only practical application being an increased area in which to stand when it rains.

But it is a major part of the architect's original design for the house. We decide, with some trepidation, to proceed, afraid we might be getting in over our heads, over our heads financially, as well as in terms of energy. We have had to exceed our "not to exceed" cost estimates several times. In an old house, nothing is certain. A three-inch brown spot on a fascia board, for instance, may indicate a three-inch spot or rot — or it may hide a five-foot span that goes into the rafters. And it is usually the latter. I hear echoes of Charlie's fears in my own ears. What if he was right?

Before we can begin on the porch, however, we have to sand-blast the entire first story of the house. The limestone blocks that make up the first story have been painted white, and we want to return them to their natural blue-gray color for aesthetic reasons; but also because moisture build-up under the paint tends to eat away the stone. (Paint seals porous rock. Moisture stays inside, causing crumbling.) The sandblasting company tells us they will need three days to do the entire house. Susan says there will be a little mess, but I am not concerned. I am far more worried about the cracks in the plaster walls and ceilings, caused by a shift in weight in the top of the house when the new roof and chimneys were added, than I am about any mess.

## June 27

The sandblasting company has come and gone. The three-day sandblasting job stretched out to two and a half weeks because the company did not do a test blast. The paint was latex; the limestone, crenelated, pitted, and scoured; and the paint would not come off. The company lost its collective shirt. I nearly lost my mind.

To sandblast, they move in a very large air compressor, which roars away at about eighty decibels, nearly the noise level outside at a jet airport. They also bring in enough sandbags to keep the Mississippi River from flooding in a two-block area, and a large hose and nozzle. Then, with the aid of the noisy compressor, they spray all this sand, which is very fine, like gritty talcum powder, out of the hose, through the nozzle, at the house. The sand hitting the house makes a loud whooshing noise, which can be heard over the roar of the compressor. The hose operators wear ear plugs, which should have told me something, but the plugs are small, almost invisible, not like the earmuff headsets worn by jackhammer operators, and I don't notice them.

Susan talks to the neighbors about the mess and the noise. One neighbor will be gone for the duration of the sandblasting; the other is very understanding — believing, as we do, that we are in for a minor inconvenience of short-term duration. We think sandblasting is something that affects only the outside of the house, that apart from the noise, it won't really interfere with our lives . . . but . . . the windows are leaky. In one case, there is an undiscovered one-eighth-inch gap between the glass and the check rail, and the house fills up daily with what looks like smoke, but what are, in reality, tiny fine grains of sand that adhere to whatever surface they land on. I throw sheets over the furniture, but do not know enough to tape the windows, since I don't know where the stuff is coming in. There is grit everywhere on our newly refinished floors. We can't touch any table, any surface, without feeling as if we have been running our fingers around the inside of a dirty ashtray. And the noise is literally deafening. Because the paint isn't coming off, the company sends over an extralarge compressor, so big it is the size of a truck and has to be parked in front of the house, rather than in back by the garage. The noise is so loud that when I go out to the car, slashes of pain shoot through my ears, and later my ears are clogged, as with a cold. And this goes on for nineteen days straight.

The noise becomes incessant and demanding, the whine of a snowmobile, a power mower, and a chain saw all at once. Escape is essential for all of us. Charlie goes to the office every day, and I arrange for the children to be elsewhere. I take frequent walks around the lake. Hurrying in the morning so I can get out of the house, I throw the beds together, leave the previous day's accumulation of debris, books, toys, papers all over the floor, put on no matter what clothes. I feel that I will pop out of my skin. My head buzzes; my jaw aches from the days of clenching my teeth. Putting my hands over my ears, I race downstairs, grab Aggie's leash from the drawer, and hook it to her collar. Smiling through those clenched teeth, I greet the workers, leave messages. Someone, I hardly know who, asks me a question; there is a minor decision to make. I answer abruptly.

"Yes, go ahead." I cannot stop to consider the merits, demerits, or implications of the situation. A perfunctory "yes" is all I can manage. Susan stops me.

"How *are* you?" she asks solicitously.

I know my eyes are staring, my motions jerky.

"Fine," I say, again showing the grimace that is all I can manage in the way of a smile. "I'm just going to give Aggie some exercise."

Jerking the dog, I start to run, fast, but the weather is hot and humid, the air so thick that the slightest movement through it releases moisture, like the pressure of a finger on a saturated sponge, and I have to stop and walk slowly, breathless. The smell of vegetation is strong: rotting algae along the lake shore, moldering grass, honeysuckle. I feel I can't breathe. My head aches at the temples. I am both hungry and full and cannot decide what to do with myself. I stare at the lake for a while, then go to the supermarket and dawdle for two hours over the frozen fish, too far gone to think of solutions. Finally I drag myself home again.

I try to leave the house for longer periods, but I can't be away for too long because there is the necessary constant cleanup. We have to live here, eat here, sleep here. Besides, four carpenters are still at work, and I have to be around at least part of the time. Working with all the noise is wearing for them, too, and they grow irritable, like me. We can't plan. Each day we think might be the last, that the sandblasters will try something new, something that will work. But there are no miracles. The paint comes off slowly, slowly. I grow so tense from the incessant noise that I have trouble going to sleep at night. Maybe I will lose it, go around the bend, like Mrs. Pruitt, the dark lady in the basement, be witness to history repeating itself. And then, just as I begin to think I might end up in the hospital, it is over. They are finished. I can sleep again.

When the sandblasters leave, I spend a week cleaning up. We can't just vacuum the stuff up — it sticks to everything. We have to vacuum, then wash. Twice. The woodwork, walls, floors, furniture, cupboards, dishes, silverware, glasses, everything. I tear a muscle in my arm trying to vacuum the wall with an industrial vacuum that has more suction than the regular one, but that weighs twenty-five pounds. And then, finally, when the house is relatively clean again, the stonemason arrives and takes his saw and begins to rout out the grout between the stones, and it starts happening again, the house is filled with smoke and I begin to rave like a maniac. I rush outside and grab the saw from the startled stonemason's hands, yelling, "Stop! Stop! I can't stand it. You can't do this. I can't go through this again!" Roald is definitely taken aback, but seeing my distress, helps me find the window cracks I had missed. Together we tape the windows inside and out, and the dust is minimal this time. I do not know how people live in areas where sandstorms are endemic. Living with floor sanding was nothing compared to this.

## June 29

It's official. The morning paper heralds this June as the rainiest ever, and the meteorologists started keeping records in the 1890s. We have further evidence to prove it. Among the detritus left by the sandblasters is silt, which unnoticed, has filled up the window wells outside. When I come down to the kitchen this morning, I notice a dank, rank smell coming from the basement. Sure enough, we are flooded. Six inches of black water cover the basement floor, turning it into a dungeon of nightmarish proportions. The water has been draining for several hours already; we can see the high-water mark about two feet from the basement floor. We can also see the problem with the window wells almost immediately, and since it is relatively easy to remedy with a shovel and a strong back, it doesn't upset us unduly. What does upset Charlie, however, are the big, dark, damp blotches on the walls above the high-water mark. Clearly, some water has been seeping in *through* the walls.

Now generally Charlie is a master of what Henry James called "the unattainable art of taking things as they come." Not me. But this time, he is genuinely distressed. He cares, really cares,

that things look as good underneath as they do on the surface
— things like chrome rods on engines, for instance. I don't
care if the bolts are rusty as long as the engine works. He
will take off seven layers of wallpaper to expose the cracked
plaster beneath. I will just slap another layer on over all the
rest.

This is the same thing, I think, convincing myself with bra-
vado. If we have a few areas of damp stone in the basement
after big rains, it doesn't mean anything. The house has stood
for almost one hundred years; it's not going to fall down now.
So we'll use a dehumidifier once in a while.

But Charlie can't be dissuaded. He can't live with a house
unless everything is just right, and the multitude of things
wrong with this one is getting to him. This is not one of the
small restoration projects he loves. This is beginning to be over-
whelming. He snaps at me.

"And we had to go and leave a *good* house for this pigpen!"

I can't say what I really feel, which is, You're right. This is
really awful. Sometimes I can't stand it either. Maybe we made
a mistake.

No, I can't admit that, even to myself. And I take his pigpen
remark as an attack on me, a rebuke for having gotten him into
this mess, and I think, That's not fair. You agreed, and you
agreed that our goal was not perfection. And I reply by defend-
ing this house and attacking the old one as if that were the
issue, and soon the fur and the feathers are flying, as we expand
quickly into cost overruns (almost three times what we had
anticipated), and who is going to pay for what, and how. And
all this before we've had our morning cup of coffee. Finally, we
simmer down with some acknowledgment on both sides that
we are indeed in a mess, and get into some productive discus-

sion about drainage ditches and sloping the land away from the
house, which we will do the next year in conjunction with
building a garage — the Dream Garage. We will simply try to
cope — and hope — until then.

Charlie builds some rain deflectors out of plywood which he
installs at critical points over the window wells on the south
side, and they prove to be very successful stopgap measures.

## July 1

Good news! The carpenters have finished their work on the
main body of the house! Gone are the sags on the north side,
the brown rot on the fascia boards under the roof, the gap-
toothed balcony railings. In their place are straight, new roof
lines and decks, and new railings, which make strong new horizontal lines. No longer gap-toothed, the vertical struts on the
balconies march in straight and regular formations that contrast
with the curves of the fish-scale shingle siding.

We have a real sense of accomplishment and strong feelings
of gratitude toward the carpenters and, especially, toward
Susan, who coordinated everybody. To celebrate, we decide to
fill the pool and give a party. We have kept the pool covered
because of all the debris, wood chips, nails, and sawdust that
have been flying through the air. We take off the winter cover,
expecting to see something that looks vaguely like swimming
pool water. Instead, we are confronted with a muddy mess, so
black that two ducks mistake it for a pond and fly in to settle.
Aggie races frantically around the pool, barking and barking.
The ducks are unperturbed. We have to drain and clean and
refill the pool, so by the night of the party only the deep end
is partly filled with icy cold water. We all jump in anyway.

The carpenters bring their spouses and friends. Harold brings his two children, one still a toddler, and Kate has her first baby-sitting job. Harold has brought his ukulele. Art has his banjo. We sit outside in the balmy air and sing the night away.

I am left with a feeling of sadness, for these are people who have shared in, and survived, all the upheavals of the past few months. They were as excited as we were when the windows were uncovered, the trim and shingles revealed. And as sad when the rains came, and the house leaked inside. And as mad when the sound of the sandblasting threatened to drive us all crazy. Some of them we might never see again. Frank is going to Germany, Art to medical school. Susan, Harold, and Paul will come back later, to work on the porch and do the painting, but this is the end of a major phase, and we are sad to see them go.

And glad, too. July and August promise to be relatively lovely and quiet. Only Roald, the stonemason, an old friend who has done work for us in the past, and two college kids who strip and scrape paint on a part-time basis, will be in residence, and they don't come into the house much.

## *July 2*

This afternoon a phone call comes from a local paint company, the public relations department of which has been looking at photographs of interesting houses that will be painted this year. Would we be interested in having our house appear on the cover of the company's annual report? We will have one day's

inconvenience, and in exchange, the company will supply all
the paint for the exterior of our house. Is that or is that not a
deal? Decision time: one second. Done!

Now comes the fun part, the part I've been waiting for all
these months, the sunshine behind the storm clouds, as it were.
I spend two days touring restored areas of the Twin Cities,
camera in hand, photographing color schemes that seem possible and attractive. I further research Victorian paint colors,
Rookwood, Downing, Devoe, and Renwick, and study their
current manifestations in Sherwin-Williams and the Williams-
burg colors. I trace the 1910 photograph of the exterior of the
house — six times — and color it in with six different color
combinations in modern colored pencils, green-gray, rose gray,
brownish gray, and so on, but the blue-gray of the limestone
first story always asserts its dominance, and we decide to match
it as best we can for the body of the house even though paint
scrapings viewed through Susan's microscope show the original
color to have been a kind of muddy green. The scrapings also
reveal at least twelve coats of paint colors on the house, ranging
from pea green to various shades of gray, to an apricot, and a
brown, to white.

The actual window frames of Victorian houses were always
painted a very dark color, usually black, so that the rest of the
house and trim colors could be changed without changing the
window colors. So, on Susan's advice, we choose a very deep
green, almost black but with a little more depth, for the sash
color. That leaves the trim color. I originally thought that a deep
grayish blue would contrast nicely with the light bluish gray of
the body color, but in the colored sketches, the dark trim looks
heavy, glowering almost, like frowning eyebrows, and white
fits the light-and-airy character of the house — the exterior of

which, we feel, should be a prelude to the interior. In the end, we decide on a cream color. Its warmth balances the cold gray and deep green. We pick three grays and two creams and paint two siding boards and trim with each, soliciting the opinions of neighbors and passersby. We try various blue-greens for accent colors, but they fail miserably, and we end up with plain old dark gray as our accent color. We won't start painting until fall, when the porch is finished.

## July 7

Roald arrives today with his chisels and awls, hammers, and wheelbarrow. His job is to rebuild the foundation and columns of the porch, but first he has to firm up a few parts of the existing limestone terrace wall that have crumpled under the onslaught of a hundred years of rain and ice.

He makes an unpleasant discovery in the first hour. A previous owner's charming flower beds, set into the terrace alongside the wall, have allowed water to leach down through the wall and erode the mortar between the blocks of limestone, so that Roald is able simply to lift one block off another in the wall. The whole thing comes apart like pieces of a jigsaw puzzle and, of course, will have to be rebuilt in the same manner. The trouble is that only half the stone is usable, and the quarries that provided that particular type and shade of limestone closed about 1910. Some of the old blocks from the demolished porch have been used in the garden, and though picturesque and mossy in the garden terrace, they will crumble if we try to use them in the rebuilt wall and porch. The fireplace in the basement is likewise constructed from the remains of the old porch, but short of dynamite, there is no way to unstick those blocks of limestone; the mortar between them is as good as the day it was set. We will have to search for stone — Roald will use what we have in the meantime.

## July 14

We take to cruising the alleys, in our search for stone, looking for likely blue-gray piles or walls. We tap at the blocks on an old barn, talk to the historical society. "Impossible to find," they say. A neighbor in the process of remodeling her basement offers us her stone, but though it is the right color, it is the wrong size and impossible to use. Roald goes to the site of the old quarry, now government property near the airport, and as luck would have it, finds a large pile of what looks like exactly the right kind of stone. We are in business, we think. Roald spends the next day negotiating the maze of corridors of city hall trying to find someone from whom to buy the stone. No one will take any responsibility for it. City hall sends him over to St. Paul to the state historical society. They send him back to city hall. Nothing. The next day, Roald goes back to the quarry with his trailer, arriving just in time to see the last of the beautiful blocks being bulldozed under the earth by road-working machines. The limestone is being used for fill.

The next day, we contact the architect who does work for the historic preservation commission. "The stone you want was called Platteville limestone," he says. "It was the most common building stone in this area in the nineteenth century, and it underlies the whole Twin City area. You can see outcroppings near the airport. But because it is the top layer of the geologic formation, it is unstable. It deteriorates if there is nothing on

*Richard Regan*

*Elizabeth Schutt*

We are blessed with early photographs of the house, given to us by former owners. *Top:* Our house as it looked in 1910, and, *bottom*, a jolly lemonade party on the front porch, circa 1894.

*Bruce Goldstein*

Our house today, and, *opposite page,* as it was when I fell in love with it and we decided to commit ourselves to the restoration project.

*Harold Bend/Bruce Goldstein*

*Bruce Goldstein*

We found the splendor and craftsmanship of Victorian
details, both inside and out, irresistible. The half-moon
stained glass window in the stairwell was covered with
shingles on the outside. Opened up to the light, its
colors are deep and rich—purple and green, mostly, with
strands of ocher and flowers of soft turquoise. *Below:* a
detail of the flooring. The pattern is made up of interlocking hexagons of walnut, birch, and white oak, with a
handsome star at each corner. *Minneapolis Star and Tribune*

*Susan Harper*

*Minneapolis Star and Tribune*

*Top:* After months of work the carpentry is nearly finished, the stone has been sandblasted, and the new porch is in progress. *Left:* A detail of the dentil molding and fish-scale shingles after the painting has been done. The stonework at the bottom right has the old-fashioned raised beading.

*Elizabeth Schutt*

*Bruce Goldstein*

*Top:* "Sweet and demure" was what young ladies of 1894 strived to be. Miss Schutt's mother-to-be is on the left. *Right:* Times have changed. Three ladies of 1985 pose in the 1894 location. Katie, now thirteen, is in the middle.

*Elizabeth Schutt*

*Bruce Goldstein*

Looking properly serene, an 1894 bridesmaid stands for her portrait on the front terrace.

Katie on the front terrace with Aggie, thankfully no longer a puppy.

*Richard Regan*

*Bruce Goldstein*

*Top:* The front hall as it was in 1910, before electrification and redecorating. This is the mostly black wallpaper we found behind a large mirror. *Bottom:* The front hall as it appears today. The staircase had been altered and all the lovely paneling removed in the 1950s.

*Richard Regan*

*Bruce Goldstein*

*Top:* The back parlor in 1910, before the Regans' remodeling. *Bottom:* The same corner of the living room in 1985. Chris and a friend are putting together a puzzle on the marble-topped table that belonged to Charlie's great-great-grandmother.

*Elizabeth Schutt*

*Bruce Goldstein*

*Top:* The dining room in 1894, before the woodwork was painted.
*Bottom:* The dining room as it is today, with the Victorian stained
glass window my mother-in-law stripped. It had been painted white
on the outside and walled up on the inside.

Richard Regan

Lea Babcock

*Top:* A 1910 view of our bedroom, after the Regans' redecoration. Note the newly painted woodwork and the Eastlake dresser. *Bottom:* A similar view today. Our own Eastlake bureau stands between the windows. The stenciled border above the picture rail echoes the original band of wallpaper.

*Elizabeth Schutt*

*Bruce Goldstein*

Cyclists calling on the ladies in 1894. This particular lady is looking far less sedate than when she posed for her portrait on the terrace.

Once again there is a stone front porch, and bicyclists still come visiting. I am on the left, holding Chris, who is now ten. Charlie is next to us.

top of it." I ask him if our house will crumble, and he assures
me that it will not. There are, after all, two stories on top of the
limestone, and it has already stood for almost a hundred years.
"The Platteville limestone," he goes on to say, "was very good
for basements and was commonly used even after good transportation made harder limestone available. It was permeable,
allowing moisture to move in and out."

I can tell him all about permeable.

"If you don't mind a dark splotch on the wall now and then,
it's still good for basements," he says.

Dark splotches are okay! I can hardly wait to tell Charlie.

"The state historical society used to have a pile of this Platteville limestone," he continues, "but it started to delaminate; the
layers started to separate because it was left out in the rain. I
heard that the society stored some in an old cave. Maybe they
would sell it."

This time a call to the historical society produces more information, if not the positive results we seek.

"Yes, the stone Roald saw being bulldozed was probably un-
usable for building material (but not necessarily for a wall). Yes,
we have some stone in a cave, but we're sorry. We never sell
stone. It's state property. We're not allowed to sell state property."

We learn that the historical society reopened an old quarry
about fifteen years ago for a big restoration project, but closed
it again seven years later. About the only source of Platteville
limestone is old buildings that are being torn down.


## July 20

A friend tells us about a building that is being demolished near
the old warehouse district in downtown Minneapolis. We wait

until Sunday, then take our trailer and scavenge. No questions asked.

One day we wake up to find a large pile of usable stones dumped on the boulevard next to our front walk. We don't know whom to thank for this unusual gift, though we suspect a certain friend who once, looking disheveled and disreputable after a day spent digging trees in the country, came bearing a gift of wild plums and yelling, "Fruit Man! Fruit Man!" at the top of his lungs. He so scared our neighbor that she locked the door and called the police. In any case, we appreciate the generosity and strong muscles.

Regardless of how many old stones we can find, however, new ones are what we need for the ten capstones that lie on top of the wall (seven hundred pounds apiece!) and the fourteen stone blocks for the columns to support the porch (three hundred pounds each).

For new stones, we need to find a quarry. We hear about a limestone called Kasota, which is still being produced in the town of Mankato, about seventy miles to the south on the Minnesota River. We decide to take a look, make it an outing, a summer picnic. We pile the children, potato salad, ham sandwiches, carrots, and soda pop into the car. Judiciously, we leave Aggie at home. I love the old Sioux Indian names — Kasota, Lakota, Mankato, Minnesota — and I think (as we take the longer scenic route and drive south along the Mississippi) about Battle Creek, which flows between sandstone cliffs into the river just south of St. Paul. How recent, really, were the Indian wars for which the creek was named. The last battle between the Sioux and Ojibwa tribes took place in 1861. At that time, a big fort guarded the confluence of the Mississippi and Minnesota rivers, just a few miles away. St. Paul was a town of small wooden houses, mostly shacks, and mud streets, and Minneapolis was barely a village. Just five years before, my great-great-grandfather had arrived in St. Paul from Connecticut. The next year, he would join the Minnesota Regiment in the Civil War. The industrial machine was in full motion. A bare twenty-five years later, prosperous men were putting up wedding cake houses. Talk about rapid change! I'm not sure the last twenty-five years have produced more.

Our mood is mellow and relaxed. We stop the car and have our picnic, exploring the sandstone caves around Battle Creek, imagining the events of that day in 1861. This is an excursion. It is summer. We pass fields of green corn that are nowhere near as high as an elephant's eye, but instead give us a view of rolling hills and pretty farms, one with all red buildings — corncrib, barn, house, outbuildings — that make it look like a wildlife painting. I half expect to see a pheasant perched on a wagon.

Mankato is a river town built on ledges coming down the hill to meet the river. At one time, it was a place where boats unloaded supplies onto wagons for the trip West. Now it is a town of thirty thousand, boasting a state college as well as the limestone quarries. We come upon our first quarry quite unexpectedly. White-faced Herefords and black Angus cattle are grazing at its lip, and we almost miss it, this wide cleft in the pasture land. The stone here is far too yellow for our purposes, looking like something out of the Southwest. But we are in limestone country all right. The woods are full of little piles of limestone, miniature Stonehenges, often capped with a big new stone to protect them from the rain. What are these piles? I wonder. Private supplies for repairing basements? Children's forts?

There is no doubt about the next quarry we come to. It looks like an open pit mine, with slabs of stone flung around as if by a giant's hand. We are almost mowed down between a large dump truck coming into the mine and a huge semitrailer coming out of it. Four different colors of limestone in the cliffs make up the walls of this quarry: purple, yellow, creamy white (the Kasota, as it turns out), and gray. None of them is right for our house. The gray is too dark, the Kasota too light. Too bad.

It has been a lovely day, however, and I am positively blissful when I call a Twin Cities stone company the next day to investigate a Wisconsin stone called Lannin, which is supposed to be close to the desired blue-gray color. The Lannin stone is good, hard limestone and quite close in color to the old Platteville, the man assures me. His company has its own stonecutters, who would shape the stones and hand cut the corners in the old way. Wonderful! I think — until he tells us the cost, at which point we figure we can afford to buy two stones, period. We decide to forgo the hand-cut corners. Our stonemason, Roald, says there is no reason a quarry could not cut the stone in the sizes we want. He would be willing to go to the quarry to investigate, to check the color, to see if he can arrange for transportation. So today Roald and his wife and baby are off on their own excursion — this time to Milwaukee, home of the Lannin stone.

## August 5

Some ten tons of stone blocks are delivered to our front lawn. Their color is not quite so blue as the stones on our house, but the thought of beginning our search over again is enough to quell the urge for perfection. Besides, who would ever take back ten tons of stone? It isn't exactly like returning a blouse to a department store.

Rain arrives with the stones, and it continues sporadically for a week. We rent a fork lift to move the stones, but the rain makes mud, and the fork lift can't make it up the front bank to the wall, even though we have cut a temporary road through the worst of the incline. The fork lift costs us fifty dollars a day, and every day Roald comes over and makes a run for it. We use planks, bricks, even some of our precious stones to try to get traction, but nothing works.

Finally the sun peeks through blue holes that have opened up the gray sky, and the ground dries up a bit. Roald climbs into the cab, guns the motor. The fork lift is up, up, almost over — and then it slips, slides backward again. Roald adds more bricks, turns the machine around, and tries it again, backward this time, for front-wheel drive. He is within inches of the top when the wheels spin, and he falls back down again, Sisyphus personified. On the third try, the motor roars, and he is up, up and over. A cheer rises from the neighborhood gallery that has gathered to applaud his efforts. Victory at last!

## *August 21*

All the foundation plantings around the terrace are down, mashed and trampled. Twenty feet of sod have to be brought in to replace what our temporary road has obliterated, but the wall and columns are beautiful. Roald has cemented the stones in the old style, with raised beads of mortar that outline each stone and give it definition. The new stone, lying on top of the old, looks like a boundary; it is a finishing touch, like a hat. The old stones make a kind of sculpture, they are so artistically arranged. I like to touch them, feel them, look at the patterns. Roald is an artist. One of the things an artist does is to make us see old things in a new way. Our new wall and columns are not exact duplicates of the old, but they are close, a nice mixture of old and new materials, and the patterns have their own integrity, which makes me think about the nature of the material, of the stone itself. The two columns reaching out of the wall up to the sky have their amusing aspects; until the porch roof is built, they will remain two giant phallic symbols. Now I hear reports of my mother-in-law's friends asking, "Just what *are* the Chrismans doing anyway to the front of their house? It looks just terrible!"

While Roald is constructing beautiful walls on the outside of the house, we are dealing with an increase in the rodent population on the inside. The new roof takes care of the squirrels, it is true, but the mice are proliferating. They are getting so noisy that I spend a lot of time in the wee hours of the morning staring at the bedroom wall with the aid of my flashlight. All the activity seems to be taking place *within* the walls, where the mice evidently have a maze of runways — behind the proverbial wainscoting, of course. Traps have proved to be only mildly successful: usually the bait is gone, but no mouse is found. They appear to be immune to poison. One day I think I hear a mouse orgy in the kitchen ceiling, there is so much scuffling and squeaking. The children have seen the creatures running around near the bookcases in the third-floor library, now the family room with TV and electric train, but I have not had that pleasure until today. I was sitting at my desk paying bills, when Chris called from the third-floor stairs.

"Mom, come quickly. Mom, hurry up! Please, Mom; there are six mice up here!"

I grab three pots from the kitchen and race up the stairs, eager to vent my financial frustrations on something hapless and still legitimate like *vermin*. But these mice are not slat-eyed, sneaky, ratlike vermin at all; they are babies! Gray and furry and miniature, long past the naked, pink, chewed-bubble-gum stage, but hardly suitable targets for unrelieved rage. Still, we throw ourselves into the hunt, banging down our pots, hoping to have trapped a mouse; but we need lessons from a cat. We lack delicacy and tackle like football players, crashing full length to the floor, confusing the inexperienced mice, four of which end up falling through the stair rail, landing with soft thuds on the stair treads below. Two, we pick off there, as they run blindly into the risers while trying to find a way back up. A third is held captive between the floor and baseboard by Aggie, who escapes from her kitchen quarters and bolts up the stairs in search of the activity. Aggie's mouse is badly mauled, and I throw it quickly in the toilet, hoping no one has seen me. The fourth mouse, more intelligent than the rest, has taken refuge in the linen closet at the foot of the stairs and is hiding somewhere behind the Ajax in a pile of rags. Six-year-old Chris, the only one small enough to fit under the lowest shelf, burrows in after it and emerges a few minutes later, bearing the mouse proudly in front of him, where it sways back and forth, dangling by its tail.

"Its name is Vickie," he announces, "and this other one," he continues, holding up a pan with a captured mouse, "is Mickie." Mickie and Vickie live in a coffee can in Chris's room for two days, at the end of which, one (Chris swears it was Vickie, but they were, of course, never sexed) drowns in the water dish, and the other, bedraggled and wet, gains its freedom in a neighbor's back yard, several houses away, where it will have a chance of survival. I hope it is not the mouse of the linen closet, but one of the confused babies on the stairs, for if not, it will surely find its way home.

## August 23

Today I start to take the paint off the stained glass window that belongs in the east wall of the dining room. Previous owners had not only walled up this intricate window, but had painted over the outside of it with the same sticky latex paint used on the stones. We are beginning to think about decorating now and need to see what the window will look like. We lay it out on two sawhorses under the apple tree in the back yard. I pour on a quart or so of paint remover and let it sit for a while, then start scraping — and scraping and scraping. After three hours, I have removed about half of the paint from one small end of the window, so when my eighty-year-old mother-in-law asks if there isn't anything she can do in the way of projects for our house, I jump at the chance, and turn the window over to her. Her eagerness to undertake such a project represents a reconciliation of sorts, and a great step forward, for when we proposed buying the house, she was adamantly against it and has remained dubious through the various stages of renovation. I am very grateful for her help. She works patiently for hours and hours and accomplishes more in one day of steady scraping than I would have in a week of impatient passes and swipes.

This window turns out to have roses centered in each of the two side plates, the same rose motif that occurs throughout the house, but in addition, there are other flowers — the lost lilies (I knew they would be somewhere!) — and red jewels. The colors this time are mainly turquoise and brown, with accents of yellow and pink. Inferior, to my twentieth-century eye, to the other rose-and-purple windows, this one is probably closest to what one thinks of as typically Victorian, with a richness of color and design so opulent that the twentieth century would eventually revolt against it and opt for the plain, simple, and straight. And in a way I can see why — the window seems, at first glance, to lack harmony and balance.

We have hired a decorator, Janet Connolly, whose work we admire and who likes Victorian houses, and together we discuss just what sort of interpretation we want, eventually letting the lightness and airiness of the house dictate its interior and aiming at an effect not too far removed in tone from the Brighton Pavilion. The interior decoration will show the influence of the late nineteenth century in scale, in the mixture of pattern and texture, and in the richness of color, but it will be light in palette, with a definite whimsical and contemporary air that will fit our lifestyle and family of children, dogs, guinea pigs, and birds. Janet produces materials, draws sketches. I bring them home to show Charlie; together we ooh and ahh, and choose the first ones I had seen. Both Charlie's and my mother are horrified.

"You can't use that pattern with those stripes, that wallpaper. And that other pattern — it makes me dizzy just to think about it," they say. Daughter Kate is also opposed. Mixing patterns for her is like mixing up the meat and vegetables on your plate — yuk. But mixing patterns is what we are going to do. Furthermore, we are going to cover the walls of the dining room with cloth, the same floral-and-vine-patterned material that will go on the living room sofa.

"Janet," I say on the phone one day, "I trust you. I have faith in you. Are you *sure?*" And I have to trust her because this is an area of my own incompetence, and I know it, and I am getting cold feet. What we are doing simply isn't done, not in the houses we grew up with or in the more contemporary ones our friends now live in. I am holding my breath.

We are lucky we already own all the furniture and rugs we will use. We have only to do some reupholstering. Besides the marble-topped table in her sun room, Charlie's mother has saved a beautiful Renaissance Eastlake parlor set, complete with carved swags, from Charlie's great-grandparents' house in Cascade, Iowa, and she has given us the settee and two armchairs, as well as an even earlier medallion-backed sofa she had stored in her attic. Those pieces, together with the furniture from our old house, fit in perfectly here. The scale of the Eastlake furniture is exactly right, in contrast to that of the wing chair, club chair, and sofa from our old house, which look dwarfed and tiny against the eleven-foot walls. We decide to bridge the gap between chair backs and ceiling with tall plants and a tree, such as a fig. Crossing our fingers, we send the furniture to be recovered.

## August 25

We are donating three large mirrors, measuring approximately six by seven feet each, to a local dance company, having failed to find anyone willing to buy them. One of the mirrors covered the stained glass window in the dining room; another reflected nothing in the hall. When we remove this hall mirror, we find wallpaper dating from the earliest years of the century, pre-1910, at least. We can see it in the Regan "before" photographs. Astonishingly, for in the photographs it doesn't look so very dark, the background is coal black, against which shine raised borders of gilt and roses, again, pink with pale green leaves.

We are sending a piece of this wallpaper to the Cooper-Hewitt Museum in New York for identification. It must have been hung during the Pruitts' occupancy, for the 1894 photographs show a different pattern. Was it put on in 1904, after the tornado, I wonder? Or was it part of an ordinary redecoration? The pattern seems very impressive with all that gilt, and just a bit flashy. Did it seem that way to people back then? Were the Pruitts trying to impress?

The mirrors that covered the wallpaper are very heavy, and even the athletic young dancers who come this afternoon to retrieve them have trouble maneuvering the large plates of glass. The dance company men have rigged up a pickup truck with an exterior frame against which to lean the mirrors, much like the plate glass carriers of yore. When the mirrors are affixed to the truck, however, they reflect such a broad area of the outdoors that spatial orientation becomes confused. A man approaching the mirror will think he is going toward the house when he is really walking away from it, for instance. Apparently two poodles being walked by our eighty-year-old neighbor suffer this sense of dislocation, for they attack the mirror and whirl around poor Mrs. Thompson, entwining her legs in their leashes like a Maypole. She is on the verge of toppling when one of the dancers comes to her rescue. He decides then and there that the overly large reflection might cause an accident at an intersection when an approaching car would seem to be nearing a head-on collision, so he covers the mirrors with blankets. Another elderly neighbor from across the lake chooses this minute to take up our proffered invitation of a house tour. Janet, the decorator, arrives thirty seconds later for a consultation. The children come home from school. The dog escapes, is spotted, though not rescued, by two boys perched in the maple tree next door. The phone rings fifteen times. Today is a family birthday, and we have a cake to decorate — all in the space of half an hour.

## August 27

The pace is picking up again. The paint company wants to take the picture for their annual report by the fifteenth of October, and we have a lot of preparation to do before we will be ready to paint, even though the two college boys have spent a good part of the summer just stripping paint from around the windows. Ninety percent of a paint job on a house like this is preparation. The paint is so thick it is separating from the wood underneath and must be removed with heat guns and scrapers or chemicals. We decide to use heat guns. They are faster and, we think, less dangerous than chemicals. The task is gargantuan, monumental. The carpenters are coming back to build the porch roof on top of the recently finished stone columns. A tree man will come to remove two large dead and dying trees and yank out some moribund honeysuckles. Susan returns with a large crew of painters. This time there are two women, Jodie and Rosemary. Marty, the painter of the whirling shingles, comes back, and with him, Chris Brown, the son of a friend whom I have known for fifteen years. A man comes to reopen the dining room fireplace, the flue of which has been cannibalized for use in the heating system, and soot rains (reigns?) again.

But . . . the progress is exciting and very visible. We are becoming something for sidewalk superintendents to watch. People stop by constantly, and Kate has set up a lemonade stand to turn their presence to her advantage. A neighbor offers to research our house for national historic preservation status as part of an architectural history course he is taking. The neighborhood paper is doing a story on our renovation, and a reporter comes to interview us. One funny-looking lady in a platinum wig strides right up the front walk and starts asking all sorts of questions.

"How many bedrooms do you have? How many baths? Where are they? Are the big windows new?" She says she'll make me an offer right then and there. I decline, thank you very much.

Some of the visitors ask Kate and Chris for their views on living in this old house. Their queries, usually prefixed by "Isn't it exciting?" or "You are lucky children," elicit embarrassing replies, sullen "I don't like it" and "It's ugly" comments, which in turn trigger my cover-ups. "Oh sure you do. It's a wonderful house. What about fishing in the lake? Being able to ride your bikes around it? What about the swimming pool and the slide?" To the visitor: "Ha ha, they're just tired today," or "It's just a stage." The children and I square off and glare — silently.

Some of the furniture comes back from the upholsterer. Is it too noisy? Were the mothers right? I get cold feet, start to doubt my judgment, pick a fight with Charlie. I am feeling pressured, partly because there is so much to be done to make the house relatively airtight (and that *is* a misnomer) for the winter. What storm windows have arrived have to be primed and painted (that becomes, in part, my job) and fitted, which is rather difficult because all the windows are parallelograms at best.

The kids get shunted aside. "Go look for the secret compartment," I say when they ask me to play Chutes and Ladders or Kings in the Corner. "Not now," Charlie says, when Chris asks for help on a model plane. School has started, and Kate goes off each day with pants that don't reach down to her ankle bone, and Chris's toes are curling at the end of his shoes.

The phone rings every minute. I answer. And holler. And run to fetch whomever the caller wants. It is certainly not me. I am beginning to feel battered by the agitation, the stepped-up pace. Even our bedroom is invaded when Rosemary and Jodie work on its balcony. I can't remember all I am supposed to do and am constantly forgetting things, pickups and drop offs.

All the activity is making me scatterbrained and absent-minded, about which the only thing good one can say is that it's better than being tense. Today, rather than milk, I pour coffee on Chris's cereal, which isn't so bad; but what happens with the meat loaf is almost a disaster. I put it in the oven and go upstairs to change my clothes, and I notice my rings are missing, my wedding and engagement rings and one I picked up on a long-ago trip to Scotland. I look all over the house, in something of a panic, imagining, among other things, that they went down the drain with the soapy water when I shampooed my hair. If they are not halfway to the Mississippi River, I finally conclude, then they are in the meat loaf, which I have pulled half baked from the oven, and which I am dissecting in the kitchen sink when Charlie comes home from work.

"Would you like a fork?" I offer graciously. We discover all three rings in the pile of half-cooked meat, which we squash unceremoniously back into its pan and return to the oven. We will serve a very good wine and give thanks that no one will have a broken tooth.

### September 11

Something rather odd happens today, and I am in a dilemma because of it. I am in the back yard putting primer on three

new storm windows and am feeling quite pleased with myself because I had to use only one rag to wipe my mistakes off the glass, when one of the painters comes striding
toward me, resolute and full of purpose like an adjutant bringing a message to an admiral: I am sorry, sir; we lost five
planes on this run. I snap to attention when he stops in front
of me.

"I have a problem. Maybe you can help me with it."

"Sure," I say. "What is it?" I don't even know his name, but
I have noticed this one. He looks very young, round of face,
with a smattering of freckles and an earnest manner. He is a
little brash, but definitely appealing.

"Do you think it's fair," he asks, "that Marty gets paid half
again as much as I do? I do just as good a job. I'm just as good
a painter — even better. I've watched him. I've timed myself
against him. I work faster. I'm just as neat." I notice his glances
moving from my paint-covered rag to the somewhat smudged
streaks on the window in front of us. "He shouldn't get paid
more than I do."

"But he's been in the business a long time," I say.

"What difference does that make? It's the job that counts, and
I'm doing it just as well as he does — better, even."

"Have you talked to Susan?"

"Yeah. She says that because of Marty's experience, he de-
serves more." He wants me to talk to Susan on his behalf. I said
I'd tell her what he said, but that it was her business. We contracted only with her. It was up to her what rates she paid.

All afternoon now, he's been huddling with the other painters, in groups of two or three, agitating. I think we are witness-
ing the beginnings of a palace revolt. Jim, for that's the painter's
name, is a natural leader. He's sharper, brighter, than the others. I've enjoyed his quick wit. I wonder what he'll do. Make

an informal union of the painters? Will they take him seriously?
I haven't the slightest idea.

Working with the painters is turning out to be much different
from working with the carpenters. The paint crew is much
larger, for one thing, and except for Marty and Chris Brown, I
have no sense of them as individuals. They seem right now to
me to be a lot of bodies we more or less collide with, do not
intermesh with, as we did with the carpenters. Occasionally
one puts out receptors, like Jim, and there is a meeting. I suppose that over time, we will meet the others, too. The painters
are, for the most part, young, part time, transient, and they are
picking up a few dollars before school starts or working here in
the North in the summer, going to Texas for the winter. The
atmosphere is rather like that of a youth corps camp, and it is I
who do not belong. I do not feel I know these people, or trust
them, particularly. There are as yet no connections, though if
we have a few more episodes such as this, we'll develop a few.

## September 14

Susan has stuck to her guns. The painters will continue to be
paid according to experience. I'm not sure I totally agree with
that criterion, though. One of the painters, a fellow named
Mike, has had three years' experience, so he tells me, and he
makes more of a mess of the storm windows than I do. Susan
has talked to him about it, threatened to switch him to the heat
guns, a job he abhors.

Jim is married, it turns out, and not only that, but fatherhood
seems imminent! I was very surprised when his very pretty,
very pregnant, very young wife appeared on the scene, coming
to pick him up today. They both look about seventeen, but

Susan says Jim is twenty-five. No wonder he wants to earn as much as he can.

## September 18

We have had two fires in the eaves. We weren't here when the first one happened. The eaves on the south side of the house caught fire as one of the painters was stripping the paint from the fascia board with the heat gun. He put it out with the fire extinguisher, then called the fire department just to make sure. The firemen arrived with the hook and ladder, pumper, and rescue truck, and since then we have been answering phone calls that begin with the question, "Are you all right?"

Today's fire happens again on the south side. We all run for buckets. I grab the first thing I can find, which happens to be the distilled water for my contact lenses, then run back for the pail in the kitchen that contains all the gardening tools, dumping them and their attendant dirt all over the kitchen floor. It seems that I am moving with excruciating slowness, as if I have leaden legs and am trying to run under water. Everyone is shouting. There is the terrible smell of burning wood. By the time I get to the fire area with my bucket, however, some smart person has thought to put the hose up the ladder, and the fire is out. My knees are shaking so badly I have to lean against the wall for support.

The house, of course, is such a tinderbox that any fire is dangerously close to causing a major conflagration. Even though we poked and prodded all the trim boards during the spring, replacing all the rotten ones we could find, there are some areas of rot hidden behind the boards or old mouse nests and bird nests that simply ignite when the heat gun comes too near.

## September 29

We now have had five fires. The latest was severe enough to require our pulling down some brand-new shingles to expose the burning beams underneath. Rosemary had been working on the north balcony when the shingles started burning. She climbed down a ladder, ran to the other side of the house for a fire extinguisher, saying nothing to the others over there about a fire, ran back and up the ladder only to discover that she had grabbed a *used* extinguisher. By the time she got back down the ladder and started shouting for help, the fire had spread. Thank heavens Marty was here today. He had the sense to get the hose and use it. Susan was right: you pay for experience. Marty's quick action was enough to save the day — again — but this time enough is enough. We are putting a hold on any further use of heat guns on the shingles, though they may be used on the trim boards, and each member of the paint crew using a gun must have a filled fire extinguisher within hand's reach at all times. I have now been three times to the fire extinguisher store, and am riding, like a surfer, on waves of adrenalin.

## October 5

To be honest, it isn't just the fires that are causing the adrenalin to flow. It's what the chaos and confusion are doing to our family. Last night we had a bad scene, which today leaves me with a bitter taste in my mouth and the fervent wish that we had never gotten ourselves into this project.

We are about to have dinner, an excellent veal Marengo left over from a party two days before. I call Charlie and the children to the table. Chris and Charlie come promptly, but we are sitting at the table before Kate comes slamming into the kitchen, outraged because her favorite TV show has been interrupted.

"Why are we eating so late?" she grouses, yanking out her chair.

I am defensive. "Because I couldn't get it ready any earlier. I was taking you to the store, remember?"

"We *always* eat too late. You never get it ready on time. What are we having?" She pokes at her plate. "What *is* that?"

"Veal."

"I hate veal. It's disgusting. We always have veal."

We hardly ever have veal, and she knows it.

"It's gross. I bet this is tongue." She pushes her plate away. "Can't we ever have anything good to eat around here?"

"For heaven's sake. Just try some. It won't hurt you. It's good. Yummmmmmmm."

Now it is Charlie's turn to enter the fray. "Mom made all this good food. You can eat it. Be nice," he says.

"Yeah, Kate," says Chris.

"Shut up, Chris!" she says, moving a piece of meat around her plate with her fork.

Charlie turns to me. "The painters forgot to clean up again. I found a paint can tipped over by the fence, and two dirty brushes under the tree. Don't they ever take care of their things? I suppose we're paying for all their brushes, too. You really should be there to watch them at the end of the day. And some of them paint like kindergartners. There is paint all over the glass on those storm windows over there. You'd think they could be neater. Doesn't Susan watch them very well?''

I start to say that Aggie takes the brushes and carries them under the tree, that Susan *does* watch, but she's not here every moment, that the paint on the glass came from me, and not to be so crabby, but I'm interrupted by the phone ringing. Kate and I both jump to answer it. She gets there first. "For you, Dad, as usual," she says, handing Charlie the phone. Now three of us are up from the table. Only Chris is still seated. It is Susan calling to say we have run out of the lighter of the two gray paints we are using, the one called lark.

Oh, God, I remember, suddenly. I was supposed to tell Charlie about the paint yesterday. Now he's going to have to go out tonight to get more.

The phone rings again. For me, this time. Someone wanting to trade car-pool dates, and incidentally discuss a child who still wets the bed at age eight. When I get back to the table, Kate greets me with, "You're always talking on the phone." (Like: "You're always breathing.")

Chris asks plaintively, "Dad, will you help me with the model airplane tonight?" But he is not quick enough because the doorbell rings. It is the tree man, working late, wanting Charlie to come out and look at the maple tree and the dead poplar.

Charlie goes. God damn it. "Aren't you going to have dinner?" I ask his departing back, but the door shuts without an answer. Kate gets up and goes to the cupboard. We are like jack-in-the-boxes. What happened to dinner?

"What do you think you're doing? Get back here," I say, peremptorily, mad now at everyone. Kate returns with the jar of peanut butter, which she plops on the table in front of her.

She unscrews the lid, sticks her finger in, and comes up with a big glob of peanut butter, which she thrusts into her mouth. Then she sits back in her chair, putting her feet on the edge, so that her knees can be seen above the table top.

"Put your feet down, Katie. Right now!"

"You make awful, yukky food. No one wants to eat it."

"Too bad. Eat some salad. You have to eat some salad."

She picks up a piece of lettuce from the salad bowl and manages to flick a piece of meat from her plate onto Chris's. He puts it back. She throws it at him. "You jerk!"

"*Stop it!*" I roar. "*Stop it this minute!*"

"See, you're always mad at me, never at Chris."

Charlie pokes his head in the door. "I'm going with Dan to look at the silver maple in the Browns' back yard. He thinks it will be a good replacement for the poplar — be back in a while."

The phone rings again. I answer. I am fast losing control.

Kate pushes her chair out and starts to get up. "Drink your milk," I hiss, my hand over the receiver.

"No. I'm leaving." She starts to go.

"I'll call you back," I say, slamming down the receiver on one of my good friends.

"Young lady. You get back here," I say, grabbing her arm. "You get back here and drink your milk."

She takes a step back, then holds her ground. I grab the glass of milk and thrust it toward her. "Drink it," I order. She rushes toward me, knocking my arm. I could have tipped the glass, letting my arm go with the blow, dumping the milk on the floor to the side. Instead I hold my arm rigid, and when she hits my arm, the milk sloshes out of the glass into her face. Milk drips from her hair onto her eyelashes, into her eyes, dribbles down her cheeks into her mouth. The front of her shirt is soaked. We stare at each other, horrified.

"You threw the milk at me," she screams, pushing me aside and running out of the room, sobbing.

What if I did mean to? For a moment I am stunned. I feel awful. "No, no. I didn't mean to, Kate," I call. "Kate, come back. I didn't mean to." I start out of the room after her, but Chris has begun to cry and is hitting me with his fists. "You're so mean to her," he wails.

This is awful. The whole family is falling apart. Out of control. I can feel Mrs. Pruitt's cold breath on the back of my neck as I try to calm Chris down and begin to think of the mess on the floor. It is then that I notice that one member of the family, at least, is behaving normally. Aggie, in her efficient way, has cleaned up the mess, and I need only one swipe with the paper towel to finish the job. Tomorrow will be better.

### October 8

There is a learning curve in this thing, a rather large one, to be exact, and I suspect that were we to tackle another old house, we could do it much more efficiently — in half the time and with half the stress. We would finish the floors last, rather than first, for instance, and live elsewhere during the period of the most concentrated work, when there is a crew about — even if we had to beg, borrow, or steal. A tent. Anything. But the way I feel today is that there will never be another old house. The next one will be tidy, small, with square corners; and it will be a place where everything works. Drawers will slide out smoothly on rollers; windows will glide up and down and seal themselves tightly when closed; doors will shut properly instead of latching themselves halfheartedly and requiring a shoulder block worthy of a tackle to complete the job; the floors will not tilt; objects will not roll away and lodge in inaccessible corners under heavy chests of drawers, children and husbands will smile. But I know that if I really think about it, I would never want to go back to a small square house, and by tomorrow I'll be singing a different tune. We will never find the space and airiness of this house in something modern. I am sitting now in the kitchen, and the light is pouring in through the big south window. The Victorian clock on the wall ticktocks comfortably with each swing of its brass pendulum, and with the slightest bit of imagination, I can conjure up the smell of gingerbread baking. A little more, and I see a stout cook with a long white apron moving briskly around the kitchen, her petticoats rustling as she pats out dough for sugar cookies.

Such pleasant fantasies are a refuge and an escape. I conjure them up to remind myself of why we are here and engaged in this crazy business. Sometimes even the fantasies won't hold . . . the cook surely would have burnt the cookies. Reality is the whine of chain saws that intermittently drowns out the soft ticking of the clock, and when the saws stop, the sounds of one of the three radios that are playing for the painters. At least here I can hear only one. When I can hear all three, it's cacophonous. Mike likes rock, Steve likes classical, and Rosemary favors country and western.

## October 9

The house is beginning to look beautiful, now that half of it is painted. We had originally decided to use two shades of gray, the darker on the third story and the lighter on the second, but somehow the colors were reversed on the first large area that was painted, the south deck and front bay. Not wanting to paint it over, I convince myself that it will be all right, by thinking of the castle in Disneyland where the color shades from dark to light, making the castle almost disappear into the sky. "Besides," I ask myself, "light gray? Dark gray? What does it matter?"

I am wrong. It does matter. The light gray pulls the wall out, and the dark gray pushes it in, so that this paint scheme has the wrong effect. Instead of accentuating the house's curves and bays, it flattens them. It takes a day to realize this; then I have to face the painters Monday morning and say, "Well, folks, I made a mistake. You have to do the front of the house over."

They take it calmly; only one is callous enough to make a joke about its being "a woman's prerogative to change her mind," and he probably thinks he is being kind, so it isn't too awful; but I feel like an idiot and consequently am skulking around trying to be invisible.

I am also trying to be invisible because of the furor caused by the disappearance of Charlie's grandfather's gold watch. The watch was, he thought, on the middle of his dresser, next to an alluring 1910, framed, sepia-toned photograph of the house. The watch is missing. We search for two days, then tell Susan, who is in charge of all the painters. She calls a meeting in our back yard. No accusations are made, no recriminations voiced, but the atmosphere becomes a little tense as people begin to distrust each other. We are all very uncomfortable.

Two days later, Charlie finds the watch on the third floor, under the bed, where he left it when he took a nap up there. We apologize to everyone, and I feel terrible. There is no one

among the painters who would steal, but we did not know them
well enough then to believe that.

## *October 13*

Today we have our seventh and last fire. No more heat guns,
period. The painters are virtually finished stripping, so nothing
is lost.

One of the painters is lost, though — or rather he's gone. I'm
not sure it's any loss. Mike, who was so sloppy, never did
reform, in spite of repeated warnings and periodic banishments
to the heat guns. Today, Susan finally had to let him go. He
took his radio (no more rock music — yea!) and said he was
going someplace warm. Florida or Texas. He tried to get one of
the other painters to go with him but had no success.

Today also — it is a big day — I get involved in yet another
imbroglio with the painters. I walk into the kitchen to find Rosemary and Jim at the kitchen desk, ostensibly studying paint
chips for color matching. Rosemary is wearing shorts, and Jim
is sitting in the chair, his arm around her bare knees. Rosemary
leans over him, slowly massaging the back of his neck.

I clear my throat. Hard. They continue their discussion in
slow, mesmerized, dreamy voices, oblivious. No paint chips
ever before provoked such a hypnotic spell, I think, as I watch
Rosemary's index finger slowly slide a paint chip along the
counter, a snail making its way along a leaf. Her voice is
breathy, barely audible.

"Too pearly, don't you think?" The words come out slowly,
like thick syrup from a bottle.

I clear my throat again, hoping the massaging will stop. Anything to relieve the discomfort. I am thinking hard of the pretty

young wife, and I am in a quandary. Should I turn abuptly on my heel? Leave discreetly? Make a big deal? I am hardly Jim's mother, after all.

Taking a deep breath, I plunge in. "Listen," I begin, then start again. "Listen. Clearly your minds are not on the subject of paint chips."

Jim's hand flies from Rosemary's knees to his lap. Rosemary straightens up, but doesn't look at me. Neither does Jim.

"How did you know?" she asks softly.

How do I *know*? They've only been touching and patting each other all week. Rosemary's hand just grazing the back of Jim's as she makes a conversational point, a touch on the sleeve here, a long meaningful look there. How do I know??

"You are pretty obvious," I say, "and if I've noticed, others have too, or soon will." I try to say it gently, but the color is rising fast in Rosemary's cheeks. I leave the room quickly.

## *October 14*

Rosemary quits today, saying she has to return to school. I am somewhat distressed. She has really been pulling her weight since the big fire. And so has Jim, for that matter. Oh me! What we don't know about other people's lives and where we've touched them. What am I to the two of them, anyway? Employer to employee? Friend to friend? How much easier it is to think in terms of a company policy: "Employee romance is out if it causes tension in the work atmosphere or affects productivity." And if that is the case, the words follow automatically: "And that's the way it is, folks. You have transgressed, and out you must go. I'm sorry. This is our policy." Simple. Clean. Neat. And no contact. No responsibility. Nothing that touches or admits to any feeling. I don't like being in the middle!

The paint is finished on the south side of the house, and it is time for the paint company to come to take the photograph for their annual report. We had been hoping the photographer would use one of our painters for his model. Christopher is the perfect candidate, we think, clean looking, bearded, blond, six feet tall, good sense of humor; but no, only a professional model will do, says the photographer. We think he is crazy.

A six-foot-four-inch Greek god appears at our front door at 8:00 this morning, carrying a set of pristine, unblemished, white painter's pants and three different plaid shirts on hangers. The model (for that's who he is) disappears into the downstairs bathroom and emerges half an hour later, reeking of perfume and wearing overalls so new and stiff that they make snapping noises as he walks. In his hand are a brand-new brush and a shiny new paint can that will never hold paint. Chris would never do. Authenticity is sloppy.

The photographer arrives. Our crew moves the scaffolding into our neighbor's yard so it faces the south deck. Clambering up the scaffold, the photographer and his two assistants sight the cameras and signal the "painter," who appears on the third-floor balcony, brush and can in hand. All is ready.

Click, click, I think, and it will be all over.

Not at all. The crew is here until 4:00. There are "adjustments" to make. First, our painters have to "unpaint" the cream trim on the roof gable, by painting gray over half of it, so it will look as if the painter is' actually in the midst of the job. Second, the bluish plaid of the painter's shirt isn't right; it doesn't offer enough contrast, and the model has to change into the orangish plaid. Filters are changed to highlight the contrast between the gray of the house and the blue of the sky. The photographer agrees to take a picture with my camera, to record that day for posterity, since I am afraid to go up on the shaky scaffold, which is already overcrowded; but he is very grumpy and keeps disappearing. I learn later that he had stomach flu and had been leaving to throw up in the bathroom.

The house is looking wonderful. We decide to paint the vertical bars of the balcony railings a dark gray in order to emphasize the horizontal railings, which are cream colored, and this has the serendipitous effect of accentuating the balconies themselves. The house grows more graceful looking every day.

*October 25*

"A Victorian lady getting dressed up for her Centennial" is the delightful way our neighborhood newspaper, *Hill and Lake Press,* characterizes our house in a two-page article on our restoration. "Preserving living history" is what it says we are doing. Recognition like this makes the project seem worthwhile even when the fatigue and constant hassle grind us down. Sometimes, however, the recognition can come too close. Getting dressed in our bedroom this morning, I glance out the window to see a whole class of sixty students standing outside, regarding the house intently, while their teacher points up — right at me — as he explains the details of the bays, dormers, and moldings of the house. Hands crossed like Eve, I take three quick jumps backward into the closet, but not before I hear one

of the students exclaim, "Oh, there's someone! And she's looking at us!" I know now what the monkey in the zoo might feel
if it had any self-consciousness.

*November 2*

Some of the new thermal-paned storm windows arrive, and
when we try to install them, they fall right through the window
frames onto the dining room floor. The windows will have to
be sent back to be fixed. Charlie looks at it as yet another episode in the Browning Sash Saga. I am hysterical.

We have contracted with the Browning Sash Company to
make the vacuum-sealed, double-glazed storm windows for all
the windows in the house that do not go up or down. These
include the half-moon stained glass window on the stair landing, as well as the two smaller stained glass windows under it,
the dining room stained glass window, the two 7-foot picture
windows in the front and side bays of the living room, and at
least three other stationary windows spotted throughout the
house. The salesman, a pleasant, dark-haired fellow named Joe,
came to measure the windows way back in June. Last week,
with no windows yet delivered, the salesman called to say the
company has made three windows, but he is sorry, they cannot
possibly make the half-moon window. We are upset. It is November; it is getting cold; the storm windows have to go on
*now*. Susan asks if they still have the pattern, the template, for
the half-moon window.

Well, no, they don't. They are terribly sorry, but they don't
know what happened to it.

"Well, would Joe mind coming over and making another, sort
of as a favor for not having told us for three months that they

could not make the window, and winter is coming fast, you know?"

"Well, yes, Joe can do that."

So Joe comes over and measures again and makes another template out of cardboard. In the meantime, we try to install one of the two small finished windows and discover the discrepancy in size between the window and its opening. The second small window also falls through onto the floor. Starting to become suspicious, Charlie thinks he had better check the newly made template before we take it over to Sam, the window man at the hardware store. All alone in the house, he tries to maneuver the extralarge, heavy metal ladder that will reach the twenty feet up to the stained glass half-moon. The ladder is too heavy; he loses control, and the tip of the ladder crashes into one of the two small stained glass windows flanking the large one, breaking the central pane into six pieces. He is sorry. The window can be fixed, he thinks. He thinks. . . .

But I am furious. These windows are my babies, my loves, and like children, they are irreplaceable. I have spent hours, days, weeks of vigilance, trying to protect them. All spring and summer, every time I heard a ladder on the south side of the house, I would jump up from whatever I was doing to make sure that there were at least two people on the ladder, that they were being careful. I have guarded those windows. And now my very own husband, my best beloved has done me in. I feel like a porcupine, stabbed in the underbelly, my unprotected side. And I am angry. And not sympathetic. And not generous, the way Charlie was to me when I ordered the wrong kind of lumber. The window can be repaired, but it will never be the same. If we use the old glass with its special qualities, it will have seams on the flat side of the circular pane. If we use new glass, its color and texture will clash with the old. That Charlie found that the template is, indeed, erroneous, means nothing to me, nor does the fact that he feels very bad about the accident. It is a bad night. We go to bed each hugging the far edges of our king-size bed. I remain truculent. No kiss and make up, for me. It is sad. Too bad.

But morning is much better. We take the window to the glass fixer, deciding to use the old glass. He assures us the cracks will be minimal. Maybe the windows are to me what basements are to Charlie.

A few days later, the big picture windows are delivered, four hundred pounds of them. Two muscular giants carry them in, grunting and swearing. These windows, too, are too small. That idiot, Joe, has measured every single window from the inside of the stops, not from the outside. The giants have to come back, retrieve their windows. Browning Sash will put a strip on them, charge us less; but the windows will have to be repainted; and the lesser charge isn't less enough. I want to sue, but Charlie dissuades me.

## November 4

One evening a reporter from the Minneapolis Sunday paper calls. He has seen the *Hill and Lake* story, he says, and has long been interested in our house, which he sees on his daily jogs around the lake. Could he do a story for the "House and Garden" section? Charlie and I debate the issue of privacy—neighborhood is one thing, but the whole city? — then invite the reporter over the next day.

I am nervous; the reporter seems to me to be abrasive and very fastidious. He clearly dislikes dogs, for instance, and keeps shrinking away whenever Aggie approaches him, and a mouse runs across the floor of our bare living room just as he is asking me about our motives for undertaking this huge project. Now, motives are complex and hard to explain. I take a stab at it. For me there are memories of childhood tied up in my grandmother's house, which was built in the same year as this one and which shared many of the same features. The beauty that lay just beneath the surface, needing only a push to become fully realized. The desire to share in one of Charlie's restoration projects, and a love of history, the feeling I had when I walked on a road in France that had been built by the Romans. We were flying like birds in the sky, but we were still walking, too, and on the very same stones that had been laid there and walked on fifteen hundred years before. Caesar's legions tramped then; ours do the same thing now; only sometimes, if we are lucky, they tramp on the football field or in the board room. I like living with history. It gives me a feeling for what lasts and what doesn't.

I try to explain all these things to the reporter, and as I wend my way through the many levels, I lose both myself and him, and that infernal mouse runs across the floor just as he is asking me whether I expect him to *believe* my explanations. "They seem entirely too altruistic," he says.

*Altruistic?* Who said anything about altruism? I shoot back an angry rejoinder and a purely selfish justification ("I fell in *love* with it"), which will give him one of his best quotes; but I am sure he is going to roast us for conspicuous consumption on the exterior of the house and vermin infestation in the interior.

## November 9

The very sympathetic, even flattering, story appears today. Eight photographs, two full pages of copy. We are calling it our advertisement. There is a picture of Kate at the piano, one of Chris swinging from the newel post. We are delighted, but the children are completely indifferent. I thought they would like seeing themselves in the paper, that somehow the news story would make them feel more a part of the project. In truth, I hoped that the article and its attendant, though short-lived, fame would help soften their antagonism to the whole restoration project, the move, and by extension, to us, the parents and omnipotent controllers. The effect on the children is certainly one of the more painful aspects of the whole job.

When we tackled our first house, working on it over a period of almost five years, we had no children at all until we were almost finished; and then it was only one baby, who didn't know plaster dust from a cloud in the sky. This time, although we anticipated the effects of the disruption of the move itself, we have not anticipated the deleterious effects that eight months of continual disruption, workmen wandering in and out, the constant moving of furniture would have on our children, often via our own stressed and irritable psyches.

Enduring a mess for eight months, or several years, does not seem unbearably onerous to us when we weigh it against the end result, because from the beginning, we can visualize the beauty of the finished product. A child cannot do this. Only the present is concrete; the future is amorphous. A child's sense of the passage of time is different from ours. A year is a lifetime, a minute an hour. For them Christmas arrives at a snail's pace, when to us it is coming at a gallop. We are talking about taking two years to complete the major work on the house. In two years, our children will have metamorphosed into entirely different people. How can we expect them to look forward to something they can't imagine when they don't know who they will be?

Now Kate is nine, at an age when she needs things to be clear, precise, and unmuddled, especially times. She will tell me she went to bed at 8:57 and got up at 6:44. No sloppy "nines" and "quarter-to-sevens" for her. It is never enough for me to say, "I'll pick you up before dinner." She needs to know, and insists on knowing, the exact hour and minute that I will be there, 5:45, for instance; and if I arrive at 5:40 or 6:00, she becomes anxious. And here we are, muddling through, never knowing exactly when a project will end or when the next one will begin, never knowing who will be around that day, where the mess will be, and when it will be cleaned up. "We hope to get this ready before winter," we'll say, or "sometime in the summer." Those words mean nothing to her, only the insecurity of not knowing. With no date affixed, it can go on forever. She is just old enough to imagine that there *is* a future, and that it is tangible, not just "when I am older" or "when I grow up."

And her room isn't totally finished. Although the wallpaper is up, the woodwork for the most part finished and back in place, some of the doors and two of the corner blocks are out being refinished, and the windows are apart. Charlie will make a window operational, for air, but he will not replace the stops and screws until he has put in new sash cord and pulleys; the time lag can be weeks. The painters are climbing in and out of her windows to get to the balcony off her room. It isn't a sanctuary. And Kate needs order in her surroundings as well as her hours. Her toys go on certain spots on shelves. Her clothes are categorized and neatly folded in drawers.

Chris cares less about order and not at all about how things look. What enrages him is the casual moving of a toy he has deliberately put somewhere. In this place of constant shuffle, such things occur daily.

Perhaps what bothers him even more, however, is the shrinkage of the special father-son times he used to enjoy so much. In the old house, for a little while after dinner and dishes, Charlie and Chris would disappear to the basement, where they would work on "projects" like chopping wood, making model airplanes, cracking black walnuts. Not any more. Charlie is a very conscientious father, but there is not much place for Chris when the project at hand is taking apart seventy-five-pound windows. Recently we have noticed an increase in demand for model-making assistance and, more ominous maybe, an insistence on precision and perfection that barely covers the anxiety underneath.

Our family conversation time has been reduced to a minimum. Usually the dinner hour is the conversation hour. The children tell about their days — what things, both good and bad, have happened to them. It is their time for their father's ear. Mine has usually been bent for several hours before. Since the work began in earnest on the house, that leisurely pace has disappeared. I compete with the children for Charlie's attention. Five decisions have to be made between 5:00 and 7:00 every night. Our conversations have become brief and truncated, exchanges of information only. "Will we use the one-eighth-inch trim or the one-quarter-inch? Repair with plywood or birch? This shade of green or that for the windows?" They are "no frills" conversations, bone to bone with no cartilage for cushioning. No "How's your ulcer?" or "Weather cold enough (hot enough, rainy enough) for you?" And no room to sense if there has been a misinterpretation, no room for an error in delivery, no room for corrections. Just the basics. Computer to computer. The children try to break in, are hushed, admonished. Big decisions we make by meeting or phone during the day, but the little ones accumulate and avalanche, typically, at dinner. The general level of tension has been high, also, making for short tempers and impatience all around. The result is more defiance and rebellion in our children, less cooperation than before.

The newspaper article doesn't help. In fact, it exacerbates the situation, because my efforts at justification — "Look! This proves that what we're doing is important!" I say, slapping the paper — only serve to accentuate the differences between them and me and cause each of us to dig in a little deeper. Finally one night, when we are putting Kate to bed and saying good night, she starts talking.

"I hate this house," she says. "It's so ugly. My room is never done. Everything is a mess, all the time. Why do we always have to get *old* things? I want *new* things." She bursts into tears. "I liked our old house. I miss my old room. I don't like these window shades. They're an ugly color." Sobbing hard, floodgates down for the first time, she pours out her torrent of words. Finally I hear it, finally I hear the pain and realize then how vulnerable she is and how much I have miscalculated. I thought this would be a wonderful house to grow up in, with all its nooks and crannies and hiding places, and it will be. But these are the kinds of things I liked as a child. They are not what Kate likes, and I have been disappointed, shockingly so — realization brings shock — in her failure to enjoy them. Kate is another sort of person entirely. She doesn't like to retreat and observe, and never has. She likes to be out there in the action, in the middle of the fray, stirring things up. She will choose a game over a book any day, likes to make brownies with a friend, sell lemonade, organize parties. She might never curl up in the window seat, watching the rain, dreaming dreams — and that's just fine. I was the child in the window seat.

Since I have come to this realization, things have begun to get better. For one thing, I am starting to listen more, rather than trying always to convince. I no longer feel so responsible. Not that I have given up the role of professional convincer ("see it *my* way") entirely; that isn't in my nature, either. The trouble is that it has taken several months to see the connections between our behavior, misperceptions, and tensions and the children's.

In the best of times, we can never see the thing itself. Our vision is too distorted by lenses of various colors and sizes. Rosy or black, magnifying or minimizing, like microscopes and telescopes, they distort our perceptions. I had on one set of lenses when I envisioned Kate and Chris happily running up and down the stairs looking for the secret compartment. "Isn't this wonderful?" I'd exclaim fatuously. "Aren't we having the best time?" In fact, it was *I* who was looking for the secret compartment. The children were sitting at the bottom of the stairs, moping. After a while I put on another set of lenses that let me see only the moping and denied the laughter that went alongside, that did not acknowledge that, if the children were not looking for secret compartments, maybe they were playing hide-and-seek or making forts out of furniture on the third floor.

It has taken us months to sort out the forms, to find the patterns, to look behind the children's actions to see — ourselves. Living on the edge, living, in effect, from one crisis to another, is not conducive to seeing things clearly. Something happens; we react, over and over, without seeing what an accumulation of these reactions will do to our normal pattern of living.

To counter my own stress, I now take a "vacation day" every week. I spend the day doing something I love that is entirely unrelated to the house or to the various jobs, volunteer and otherwise, that I do. Looking at art galleries and museums, going out for lunch are for me both relaxing and stimulating in a way that is far different from the fast-paced jogs and walks that were tension relievers before. They were literal escapes, runnings away, a form of negative relaxation. I really don't like running. I have flat feet. Though exercise definitely has its place, "vacation day" has reduced the irritability to a great degree, as does the reduction in size of the paint crew. The paint job is nearing completion, and we are down to two carpenters, who are working on the porch, and one painter.

## November 14

Waking early, before anyone else, I step outside. The rain showers of the night before have stopped, but the air is still moist and misty, the sky clouded over. The wet, fallen leaves emit an odor of the forest, dank and ripening. The lake is still and clear, with fingers of mist hovering above its surface, and suddenly I am in the north woods, having just emerged from my tent on a fall camping trip far off in the canoe country. The only sounds I hear are the scrabbling of two squirrels chasing each other around the trunk of a large sugar maple and the insistent honking of a flock of Canada geese out on the island, their rookery disturbed by some intruder.

Finally, a lone jogger approaches, reminding me that I am less than two miles from the very center of a metropolis with a population of more than two million, and it is time to get moving, engage again with other lives. Yet, the moment of stillness is perfect. It will linger. I will know it is there.

And I have to remember such moments of peace, because the stairwell ceiling is showing spots of moisture again. This time we know it is not the deck that is causing them and look farther up. We determine that a design fault in the house, a too-steep saddle on the roof by the turret, causes the water to overflow and back up under the shingles whenever we get a very hard rain, a torrential downpour. We will put in a four-foot-high metal flashing and hope, finally, that we have solved this hundred-year-old problem.

## *November 30*

The carpeting is on the stairs, putting the finishing touch in the front hall, which was wallpapered two weeks before. The carpeting looks lovely. It picks up the reddish purple tones of the stained glass but is softer, lighter; and it doesn't look "pink and blue" with the wallpaper at all. In fact, the whole first floor is looking quite beautiful. I am amazed at how the rose wallpaper in the living room makes that giant space actually seem cozy. Before the wallpaper went up, we tried our Sunday night foul weather ritual, a winter picnic before the fireplace known as pizza-on-the-rug, and sitting there, huddled together in the middle of this hall-like room with its greenish white walls, made us feel cold and clammy, as if we were in some damp castle. The rose wallpaper and the flowered chintz upholstery give the room a bit of an English country house feeling, and it is very nice and warm, not noisy and loud at all. The patterns mesh, not clash; there is the feeling of Victorian richness, combining a bit of the Orient with lots of texture. The atmosphere is the opposite of sterile, which is, I suppose, "fertile," and the image fits. This house is a place in which to grow.

## December 18

The doorbell rings, sounding out the first line of "The Chimes of Westminster" — bing, bong, bing, *bong* — clearly announcing its 1950s origin in the process. The man who rang it, our eagerly anticipated visitor, lived here before the chimes were installed. He is the youngest member of the Regan family, three generations of which occupied the house from 1910 to 1945. When we removed the wallpaper in the front hall, we found his curriculum vitae scrawled on the plaster underneath:

My name is Richard Francis Regan
My mother is Philomina Morgan Regan
My brothers are Robert Morgan Regan and John McVeigh
    Regan, Jr.
We live at 2405 East Lake of the Isles Boulevard
    Minneapolis, Minnesota
    U.S.A.
    The World
    The Universe

I am in the third grade at Kenwood School
April 29, 1943

This same Dick Regan is the man responsible for sending us the 1910 photographs that provided the impetus for our restoration. It was he, too, who unearthed the wonderful letter from his grandparents expressing their joy that the house would stay in their family for another generation. Here in the Twin Cities on a visit from his home in San Francisco, he has come back to renew acquaintances and to see what use we have made of the photographs of his childhood home.

"You mean you haven't found the secret compartment yet?" he asks after we show him the other treasures we've discovered: the stained glass, the brass drawer pulls, the roses on the fireplace tile, the upside-down match holder. We follow him upstairs to Chris's room, where he removes the bottom drawer from a built-in bureau in the closet. Hollowed out in the floor underneath is a cavity, just big enough to hold a smallish child. "The perfect place for hide-and-seek," he informs us. "My brothers could never find me!"

The compartment is empty now, except for a few dust balls. I am surprised. I didn't expect it to be empty, somehow. I thought there would be at least a relic left from a previous owner, an old marble or something, maybe even letters or an old dried-out corsage. I guess it will be up to us to leave something, bits and pieces from our tenure here. A bit of fluff, perhaps, from the cat's first litter of kittens, a jackknife, the skull of a small animal from Chris's collecting years; later, perhaps, a page or two torn from his stash of *Playboys* or *Penthouses*. What I secretly hope is that when we opened it we released the ghosts of the Regan family, whose joyful presence will now emanate from this place and flow throughout the house. Maybe we can shut it again and lay the ghost of Mrs. Pruitt to rest. Never again will she come to haunt us.

### December 31

New Year's Eve, and we are set to howl. I have a new gold shirt that ripples when I move, like a second skin. I feel slinky, daring, the way I do when I wear a red dress, and thereby become brave enough to ask men to dance with me. Charlie looks wonderful in a dinner jacket and pleated white shirt with a Christmas cummerbund. I think he is elegant, like Fred Astaire. Both of us are bubbly and exhilarated, needing no champagne to set us afloat. We are already bobbing like corks on a sea.

This has been a big year for us, and now finally, we are beginning to relax. We will take a break from this restoration project of ours, the knowledge of which undoubtedly contributes to my sense of joy. We will have a quiet indoor winter, resting a while, like the animals in hibernation, maybe getting to know each other again. Though we did not quite achieve our dream of a Victorian Christmas with a fifteen-foot tree in the stairwell (contenting ourselves instead with a seven footer in the corner of a living room that is still without curtains, pictures, or fig tree), still, we have made giant strides. Susan commemorates our first Christmas by sending us two turn-of-the-century glass lamp shades dated and signed by the artist, Quezal. In the shape of bells, white on the outside, coated on the inside with pink overlaid with gold, they look luminescent, like pearls. When lit, they glow with a light warmer even than candles.

The big push is over. We worked fast, and we worked hard, and we accomplished a great deal in a very short time. It has been an adventure of sorts, this trip through time, and we learned a considerable amount, though sometimes the knowledge came with pain and discomfort, like surviving the rigors of a winter camping trip, where frostbitten toes go along with the sight of incomparable beauty. For those who survive, there is the feeling of exhilaration and a sense of growth — both are the rewards of adventuring.

When we return from our party, we turn on the radio, tuning in to a program of Strauss waltzes — "The Emperor," "The Blue Danube," "Die Fledermaus." I kick off my shoes, and we begin dancing. One-two-three, one-two-three. Soon we are whirling and twirling, faster and faster, until the music pauses, in breath-stopping rubato, then faster and faster again, our feet seemingly leaving the floor. Franz Josef's court, *La Traviata*'s Violetta had nothing on us. We dance this way for an hour, just the two of us, swooping around the bare polished floor of the old second parlor, the room that was once covered with cabbage roses. We are getting there. Next year — we'll have that fifteen-foot tree!

# III

# WINDOW GLASS

*January*

The worst blizzard ever to hit Minneapolis drops three feet of snow in as many days. Compacted by the wind and dispersed in heavy drifts, one of which stands five feet tall across our front walk, the snow makes driving impossible. We cannot even get out of our garage, much less the alley, but we are invited to a party just across the lake, and we want very much to go. We snap on our cross-country skis, put our contributions to the party — celery sticks and dip, and cheese-stuffed mushrooms — in backpacks and set off across the lake like Telemarkers of old.

The wind blows in from the northwest, almost knocking us over as we trudge across the lake, but on the way back it pushes us from behind and we skim across, our bodies acting as sails.

The northwest winds blow inside our house too. I think fondly and regretfully of those caulked and painted-shut windows that made our living room warm and cozy last winter. On the last day of the blizzard, the temperature inside our house is a chilling fifty degrees, and the furnace hasn't turned itself off once in three days. We stuff rags around the window, grab caulking guns, raid the tape drawer, and rummage through the children's rooms looking for any sort of material to put around the windows; but though the windows are now stuck with Scotch tape, black plastic tape, silver duct tape, even sticky metallic blue tape with stars, the wind still comes in, a lot of it at floor level. Charlie discovers large areas in the basement, at the juncture of the foundation and first-story walls, that can be stuffed with insulation, and the draft lessens considerably. Of even more help is the furnace man, who tells us that because our fan is not working properly, we are getting only half the air circulation we should have. He fixes the fan in fifteen minutes, and once again, we are warm.

Not long after the blizzard, the living room curtains arrive. *Curtains* is a misnomer, for what we are using are not really curtains, swagged and draped and valanced, but pleated Roman shades that match the background of the floral fabric on the sofa and, in the dining room, the floral fabric on the walls themselves. We had debated using traditional Victorian curtains, but they would have hidden the fine woodwork, and we wanted nothing that compromised, even a bit, the even finer views. Besides, our new Roman shades are lined, and when they are let down, there are four layers of material where the pleats overlap, making excellent insulation on those giant windows. We lower the shades on cold nights and on stormy days and are nearly as draft free as when the windows were caulked and painted shut.

Now the living room and dining room are almost complete. We lack only our green trees and a dining room light fixture. I spend one cold day most agreeably at a large greenhouse, where I select a fig tree to bridge the gap between chair top and ceiling near the wall at the front of the house, as well as a palm for a corner by the piano. We spend another day combing antique shops for a dining room light fixture and find a spectacular one in ruby glass, an inverted bell shape with cut glass teardrops, very 1890s, which we do not purchase because of the astronomical sum its owners are asking. We do find, however, a black wire fireplace screen, scrolled like wrought iron, that dates from the 1860s. As for the dining room chandelier, we will temporarily use a brass one, only a little too small, that we bought in France.

The marble-topped table from Charlie's mother's sun room serves as a game table in the old second parlor, which we leave fairly open, a place to gather and stand and talk. My piano sits there in the north bay, where a fringed fainting couch stood in 1894, encouraging the house's occupants to loll and enjoy the view. Our main sitting area is the former front parlor, and now we need only to hang a few pictures to give it a finishing touch. Actually, in our living room, the windows are so much a part of the decor, it is like living outside in the woods. The changing seasons provide changing pictures. Now, for instance, we have a distant landscape, the snow on the top of the Kenwood Park hill glowing pale pink in the slanted rays of winter sunlight. In the summer, our landscape is nearer, focusing on the lake, the trees and leaves blocking the view of the hill.

In spite of the large windows, however, we need something above the sofa, which rests against the wall opposite the fireplace. Charlie's mother digs in her attic again. She unearths a large canvas, a nineteenth-century seascape, two people on shore looking out at a storm-tossed sea, on which toil two small boats. It was painted by her mother and grandmother, she says. Whoever did the sea and sky was a skilled artist. The people and the boats are in a different, more primitive style. No matter. We love it, and it fits this house, where many lives have tarried awhile. A fine portrait in pastels of one of Charlie's ancestors goes over the dining room fireplace, and I think to myself, well, if he is going to have one of his relatives, I'd better have one of mine; so we hang a portrait of my grandmother — at least I think it's my grandmother. A naked woman sits with her back to the artist, her shoulders rising above a red drape that has fallen to her waist. Since I can see only the back of her head and her shoulders, I can't identify her, but her name and that of the artist are neatly penned in the lower right corner. Maybe she was his mistress. My father doesn't believe it for a minute — his mother would never do a thing like that! — but then he is closer to the days when the subject of the fertilization of trees was taboo.

### February

What I am finding out about the snow is that it has to be shoveled — off the roof! Little spots of moisture appear again on the stairwell ceiling, and when I go up to check the problem area on the deck that has produced so many such spots in the past, I find a large ice dam blocking the exit to the too-steep valley that is supposed to drain onto the south deck. Ice has backed up, too, underneath the shingles on the turret roof. Now, every time it snows, I am up there with my extralong roof rake, pulling great clots of snow down off the roof.

Today's problem, though, occurs on the west deck, the one at the front of the house above our bedroom. When the snow gets too deep, it has to be shoveled off this deck too, or it will form a layer of ice underneath, the weight of which bows down the metal deck and causes the soldered seams to break loose in tiny areas. I clamber out one of the small side windows flanking the main one, bent over double like a clown getting out of a tiny car, pushing my shovel before me. I am in the middle of my work, heaving and ho-ing, when the window slams shut behind me. These third-floor windows are ancient, indeed, without weights and held up only by small pins and springs that go through the edge of the sash into notches in the frame itself. The pin has slipped. I can't get back in the house. I am stuck here out on the deck.

I lean over the balcony looking at the lake shore below. Amazing. For once there is no one there. Eric, I think; Eric must be somewhere. Eric does odd jobs such as lawn work and snow shoveling for several of the families on this block; and he lives here besides. Eric has ladders. He is always around somewhere. I yell, "Eric, Eric," at the top of my lungs. No answer. I wait for a while and try again, leaning over the edge of the balcony, hand cupped around my mouth. "Eric, Eric, where are you, Eric?" This time a few passersby look up, curiously, at this weirdo who thinks she's Juliet. Should I ask them to call someone? Who? The police? We have not yet given our keys to the neighbors. I let them pass. But I am getting cold. I think I will have to smash the glass. I try tapping tentatively with the handle of my shovel. The glass seems awfully solid. I will really have to wham it. I raise the shovel and am about to bring it down, hard, when I get one more idea. Reversing the shovel, I jam the edge of the blade at the edge of the window, just where it meets the sill. The frame is rather rotten — Charlie hasn't gotten up here yet — and eventually the blade goes through. I apply leverage. The pin snaps, and the window flies up. From now on, I prop the window open with a book.

Although this winter is basically R and R from house projects, we are finishing up a few loose ends before we start thinking about big projects again for the spring and summer. Big, not *big*, like last year. Bedrooms, landscaping, a garage. One of the loose ends is the railing for the balcony on top of the front porch. Harold is steaming and laminating and bending the railings by hand. As we have nothing but the 1910 photograph to guide us as to their exact height, Harold brings over trial posts and columns, and we compare heights from the vantage point of the photographer, as well as from the porch roof itself. Harold is also working on casings for the dining room stained glass window. Previous owners had removed them when they installed the mirror. Harold has to make a knife with curves that will match the curves in the old woodwork, and he has to hand carve part of the top.

Charlie is taking the paint off the two giant hinges that hold the dining room door to its frame. These are swivel hinges, each eight inches long, and scrapings reveal a glimpse of shiny metal; whether solid or plated, brass or copper, we can't yet tell. Unfortunately a flange on one of the hinges snapped off during its removal. Charlie says it can be fixed. I have unearthed the trisodium phosphate, left over from work we did on our old house, and have been scrubbing the tiles around the dining room fireplace. I am rewarded by seeing that the roses are outlined in yellow and not dirty red as I had thought. The tiles are a soft, light brick red, not maroon.

I am also, little by little when time permits, peeling off layers of wallpaper in our bedroom in two corners, trying to go layer by layer to see the various patterns underneath. It is both frustrating and fascinating and compels me, like peeling layers of skin off a sunburned shoulder. I can't leave it alone. It is a minitrip through decorating history. First a dizzying pattern from the turbulent sixties which comes off in sheets, leaving its backing, a calming white. Scraping that away, I find what looks like a fishnet on a blue-gray sea. Opening the area of that layer a little wider, I see that it is not a fishnet at all, but the same pattern as the frothy paper in the closet, only blue instead of pink. Garlands of white net caught up by pink roses against a colored background. Cinderella's dress. Underneath the blue is the pink wallpaper of the closet and, underneath that, small groups of peasants dancing on a green background and, last, some English roses. I imagine this last wallpaper was put on in the thirties. Probably the second generation of the Regan family stripped the walls down to the plaster before they began their own papering, so I do not find the late-nineteenth-century patterns here; we did find one, gold spiraled circles on a cream background, behind Kate's fireplace. The two layers of Cinderella wallpaper fascinate me. What sort of woman would have wanted such a bower? Pink froth — and then the same pattern in blue. It must have been like sleeping in layers of tulle. Sugar and spice and everything nice. Illusions. The 1950s, the calm before the storm.

Looking at the wallpapers, and thinking of the times in which each was current, makes me think of the past and present images we have of ourselves and of how they change. If one image of the 1950s woman was that she was reduced to a confection, a piece of candy, still another was presented by Nancy Drew, Superwoman, and Mary Marvel, an image perhaps left over from post–World War II, running counter to the other, but foreshadowing the trends of the seventies and eighties. The architecture of our house itself expresses one image. It is idiosyncratic like most Victorian architecture. The crazy angles of the roof, projecting gables, irregular balconies, moongate all express an entrepreneurial, individualistic exuberance that says, "I can do it. I can fix it. I can make it beautiful in my own way, which is not like any other way." But such individualistic houses existed within a community of such houses like individual snowflakes within a drift, and when society became more interested in commonality, when the snowdrift became more important than the separate flakes, architects began to express what we have in common with others, not what makes us different — and we got unadorned cinder-block squares and Levittown.

These periods where a shift in image takes place fascinate me. The surface is still and calm, but underneath the waters are choppy. The Edwardian era, Mrs. Pruitt's era, the period that encompassed the time from the Gay Nineties to the First World War, was such a period. We were going from a time of reliance on the values of empire — reverence for received tradition, things eternal, hierarchical, authoritarian — into an age where nothing was certain except one's own responsibility for oneself: make of your life what you can, take responsibility for your own actions.

During the periods of calm before the storm, where the changes are taking place underneath but not on the surface, the surface becomes more and more rigid. Forms and rituals become more important as the values that produced them disappear. We can sense the ground beginning to slide away under our feet, so we hold more tightly to forms and rituals because of the promise of stability, of putting things in their places, so that we know what things *are*. Certainly it was very important in my grandmother's day to continue the tradition of calling cards, even though telephones were widely in use. Even more astonishing is that Charlie and I have such a box of calling cards, which in all probability we will never use, not even for putting on wedding presents for the children of our friends. Think of how far removed our way of socializing is from the days when ladies went calling and left their cards on a silver salver.

I think, too, of the adolescent boys who used to take me to movies, scurrying around and jumping over curbs just so they could walk on the street side of me, a practice taught them by their mothers, anxious that their sons know the proper way to behave, but a practice whose origin — walk on the outside to keep the ladies' skirts from getting splashed by mud flung up by a passing horse — had absolutely no relevance in the 1950s and 1960s. No wonder the rebellious 1960s.

And I remember the ritual Sunday dinners of my childhood, repeated endlessly Sunday after Sunday at the home of my other grandparents — great believers in family, hierarchy, paterfamilias, and primogeniture — family dinners at which even my parents chafed, dinners that dated from a more leisurely time. A minimum of fourteen people, but usually twenty, attended these dinners, aunts and uncles and cousins. We always sat for two hours and ended the meal with chocolate ice cream and marshmallow sauce, which I remember watching each Sunday as it slowly melted into a brown soup with white swirls and a little lump in the middle; because, of course, we never could start until everyone was served. Rituals, traditions, the past — what we keep and what we discard and what we revive — they all tell us something about ourselves and how we see each other now.

## *March*

Cracks. Cracks are appearing in the walls again, long and snaky, reaching up toward the front of the house. On the whole, they are confined to the third floor, though there is a bad one in the corner of our bedroom. When we had our last outbreak of cracks this summer, we determined that the causes were the new chimneys and roof, which, being slightly heavier than the old ones, caused a minuscule shift in weight and some settling. The trouble now is that I can't tell which cracks are new and which are old; I just know there are more of them. Some we tracked last summer with weekly pencil marks to see if there was a shift, like movement along a mini–San Andreas Fault; but most are unmarked, and I don't recognize them. A small wet spot has also appeared in the kitchen ceiling about a yard out from the window on the south side. It is time to call Susan again.

I am on the third floor in the middle of the Jane Fonda Workout (the easy one) when Susan rings the doorbell. I invite her to join me, and we begin where I left off, with the abdominal exercises. From the vantage point of the position for this exercise — back on the floor, legs waving in the air — we can see the cracks in the ceiling very clearly. "The keys are coming loose, too," Susan informs me between huffs and puffs. I nod knowingly, unable to speak, but proud to be a part of that select coterie who knows what the phrase means. "The plaster is separating from the lath. Your ceiling will soon fall down." When we are finished with the exercises, Susan traces some of the cracks with her finger.

"Do you mind if we go look at the basement?" she says. She pushes up sections of the dropped ceiling in the basement playroom and discovers a cracked joist. "You see here," she says pointing to another area, "the bridging is missing. This joist is turning a bit." I don't see. Can't see. Won't see. I look anyway. Just a peek. Where long ago, carpenters had removed parts of the walls to put in the heating ducts, there are open spaces that should be filled with crisscross braces held tight against the joists. These are bridges. Not too serious. We can fix that. "I think we should call in a structural engineer," says Susan, "just to check, make sure the footings are solid, that the house isn't shifting."

Oh, boy, I think. Funny that this time I don't panic, don't think Oh, my God! I do not feel like Chicken Little, terrified that the sky is falling, as I did last year each time we discovered some potential disaster. I am more familiar with this house, feel more secure, because even with its creaks and its cracks, it has stood for nearly one hundred years, and it is not tilting. And I have slept in it for nearly a year.

The structural engineer reports that the third-floor cracks in the ceiling came from the combination of first, a very sudden cold snap, and then, a very heavy snowfall last autumn, which, because of the added insulation, caused some extra weight on the roof. Insufficient footings (concrete pads) under the chimneys caused the diagonal cracks, and they will soon stop. The house is not shifting forward. It will not topple into the lake. However, the ceiling is weak in the basement underneath what used to be the wall separating the front and rear parlors, and two supporting posts would be a good idea, as the span is now too large for the amount of support in the basement. Nothing urgent. Your house will not fall down on your head, Madam. Aw shucks, I knew it all the time.

The wet spot in the kitchen ceiling turns out to be nothing

more than water seeping through a place in the bathroom floor above, where the grout has come loose. Nothing traumatic, just one of the joys of old house ownership.

### April

We are starting to make plans for the summer's work. We will do some second-floor decorating, do some kitchen work, put in a garden, and in the fall, build the Dream Garage. Janet brings over fabrics, and once again we discuss colors — this time for bedrooms, ours and Chris's. We want our bedroom to be cool, a tranquil place. Chris's has to withstand a certain amount of abuse, like balls being thrown against the walls. In both rooms, the high ceilings make two-foot-wide, Victorian-style borders above picture moldings a possibility for the walls. We can see how they would look from the 1894 photographs. We decide to stencil the border in our room, taking the pattern from one of the fabrics we will be using in the room. Chris's border we will leave white, with a series of four stripes to mark the boundary between wallpaper and border. I buy a goose down quilt for our bed, find a bunk bed that can double as a gymnasium for Chris. He loves it and scurries all over it like a monkey. He drapes sheets from the top bunk to the bottom and makes a cozy fort. He runs strings from the top bunk down to the back of chairs across the room and slides his little plastic men down them like a boatswain's chair. When I walk in his room, I have to wend my way through a cobweb of string.

Aside from taking down the wallpaper, we won't do any of the actual work on these two rooms until June, when Kate will go off to camp for a month, leaving her room free for us to sleep in. Our room will have to have a new ceiling; the old one is cracked and water damaged, and the keys are very, very loose indeed. We also need to do some work on the closet, which has sliding doors that forever come off the tracks and modern flat casing. We want to replace the casing with the same oak wood-work that is in the rest of the house. Harold can do these small jobs when he comes to work on the kitchen. We have found that the area allotted to the kitchen table is very cramped and think we can expand it by knocking out part of the wall between kitchen and back porch, using half the porch for our eating area, keeping half for a mud room. We will do the bedroom work first, leaving plenty of time for wallpapering upstairs while Harold is at work in the kitchen. Harold assures us that a month is ample time. We consider putting in a second bathroom on the second floor. It would be nice. Friends warn us about teen-agers taking showers every day. Another bathroom, though, would be very, very expensive, and we think we can make do using the third- and first-floor bathrooms as auxiliaries. Besides, we rationalize, in this day of teen-age isolation, where each child goes around with ears plugged into cassette players or watches TV alone in a room or talks on his or her own phone, what better place to get to know each other than the family bath-room? What better place to teach sharing, consideration for others? No spitting on my side of the sink. No hogging all the towels. We may end up with lines, with slammed and locked doors and huge battles, but it's worth it, I think now. The other reason is that I just can't take any more major construction.

If there's one thing I've learned from last year, it is that I am no superwoman, no being of endless stamina. I have limits, and to push myself past them is to foolishly flirt with disaster. This time there will be no big crews of people working all over the house, just Harold and a helper, and though there will be some mess, it will be confined, and the inconvenience will be short — a month. I can stand that. Easy. If we can only train Aggie.

Aggie added greatly to the confusion last summer by causing a series of minicrises that made our real ones seem even worse. "God damn it, Aggie!" I'd hear several times a day. "Come here, you son of a bitch!" and then, "Katherine, could you come? Aggie's got my paintbrush/sunglasses/hammer/glove." I'd go outside, and there would be Aggie, dancing just out of reach, glove or sunglasses in her mouth, daring someone to chase her. I'd try shutting her in the house, but someone always left a door open. Workmen stored tools and paint in the basement, extension cords ran through the doors. Whatever she took, she grasped with a grip of iron, so that even if we did catch her, no amount of pressure on her gums would make her release the object. The only way I succeeded in getting her to drop whatever she had was by offering her a dog biscuit, in effect rewarding her. Not only did she take the workmen's things, but she stole food off the kitchen counter and took the toothpaste from the bathroom; so that not only did we have to cope with the workmen's mess, but we had toothpaste coming out the middle of the tube. She hasn't reformed.

I have made many efforts over the winter to train her. A book I read on the subject suggested using noise, such as shaking a chain of tin cans whenever the dog did something offensive. I tried hiding behind the kitchen door and, when she jumped up on the counter, leaping out at her like a demented Valkyrie, clanging together the pot cover I held as a shield and the soup ladle I carried as a sword. That stopped her, cold. But I couldn't spend my days like that. Next I tried putting out on the counter some pats of butter with drops of Tabasco sauce on them. At first this technique looked promising. Aggie jumped up and chomped at one piece. She drew back, shaking her head and blowing. She did it again, with the same result. Then, angry, she sat and barked at me, and barked and barked, looking from me to the butter and back again, before finally jumping up and eating it all. The children do not help by leaving toast crusts and cereal around. When Aggie takes something, she retreats under the table and growls. I have tried to retrieve the object by poking her with a wooden spoon. She snaps at the spoon, and the children cry that watching me is like watching baby seals being clubbed to death. I tried mousetraps on the counters, but too often they went off on my fingers. I tried cayenne pepper, but Aggie ate four slices of bread coated with the stuff, and promptly threw up all over the kitchen floor. We are back to dog biscuits, and she is gentle as a lamb about relinquishing an object. She just takes them more and more often.

### Easter

This year we are awakened at 2:00 A.M., not by plunks of rain falling on the steps, but by a commotion in the living room. A crash, the scraping of a chair being pushed over the floor, a general scuffling. A burglar? Charlie grabs the flashlight. I cling to him like the vine as we cautiously descend the stairs. It is Aggie, of course, escaped from the kitchen to run riot in the living room. She has eaten all the Easter eggs, eaten every last one we put out for the crack-of-dawn hunt we always hope will take place an hour later. A pound of foil-wrapped chocolate eggs, six bunnies, a hundred jellybeans, some disgusting orange marshallow chickens. She has rooted under the sofa cushions, sniffed around chair legs, jumped up on the window seats, stolen out of ashtrays. The only places she missed are a spot in the innards of the dining room table and the strings of the piano. We drag her back to the kitchen, tail between her legs. At least she is ashamed of herself.

But what are we going to do about the Easter egg hunt? Kate had some jellybeans in her room. Maybe those and a few cookies. I search Kate's room with the flashlight and all I can find is a jar of gooey elderly jellybeans, half clumped together and pallid and sickly, their color faded by old age. We separate them and distribute them one by one in our various hiding places. Chris's sad comment, as he looks at his tiny horde: "The Easter bunny must have been very tired this year."

The Easter bunny was very tired. Is very tired. This is one tradition, I think, that has lost its soul, with which I wouldn't mind parting. I look at Chris's paltry handful of jellybeans and contrast it with the extravaganzas of my childhood. A giant Easter egg hunt at my grandparents' house. Little boys with slicked-back hair and little girls with slippery soles on new black patent leather shoes, sliding around, in and among the flower beds in the garden. The beds were old and brown then, the snow barely melted, but the first green shoots of tulips were visible as they pushed up through the straw, the first green growing things we had seen since November. We were celebrating the return of spring. We searched for real eggs then, dyed, many colored, some blown out and as light as a feather and patterned in the Ukrainian style.

At the end of the hunt, my grandfather presented each child with a huge egg coated with crystals that sparkled in the sun, an egg whose open end held a window through which we could see a little world, a garden perhaps, or skaters on a frozen lake. What bliss. But still we wished for chocolate, and chocolate is what the children get now, and the tradition has lost much of its meaning. Who can see symbolism in an orange marshmallow chicken and a foil-wrapped chocolate oval? The kids don't even associate the candy with an egg, much less the coming of spring, rebirth and regeneration. Maybe next year when we have tulip beds, we'll revive the old tradition. Or maybe we'll wait until we're grandparents.

## May

What I think is the most beautiful month of the year is here again. The sun is warm and life giving, not the pale imitation we have all winter. The ground smells nice and wet and swampy. Apple trees are in bloom. Crowds stroll by the lake again, and the blood of my agrarian ancestors rises in me like sap in the trees, and I want to get out and dig in the dirt, an ambition I can satisfy because we are in the midst of garden planning and planting.

Previous owners have done some fine terracing in the back yard. Some of the stones from the original front porch form the wall of one terrace. Mossy now and flaking, these stones are picturesque and remind me of ancient forests, promontories, waterfalls, the nineteenth-century Romantic notion of the sublime. I love these old mossy stones and insist on keeping them, despite their relative instability. They are the perfect boundary for a picturesque wildflower garden, which we will put in little by little in the shade of an old apple tree near the garage. For a beginning, the children and I drive to my aunt's farm in Wisconsin and hunt in the springtime woods for hepatica, pink and white trillium, Dutchman's-breeches, wild geranium and ferns, which are just coming up, their fronds still curled around themselves like snails. We pile clumps of these plants in the back of the station wagon and drive back to the city. I have more than enough of digging in the dirt.

The other terrace is made from newer limestone, put in, we think, in the 1960s at the same time as the swimming pool. This stone is in perfect shape and will hold up nicely once we begin digging. It is the ideal spot for a perennial garden, nice and sunny. I learned a little bit about gardens when we lived in France, but I didn't grow up with one and don't have much sense about what blooms when and how tall the various plants are; nor do I know many names. I do know I want some lilies and some roses, both for their Victorian associations and just because I have always loved roses; that is, I have always loved looking at roses in a vase in someone's house.

In Minnesota roses require a great deal of work. Once I had a few of them in a garden. To get them ready for winter, I had to dig a trench out from the base of each rosebush, then with a pitchfork, I had to lift the bush and lay it in the trench, like in a coffin. After that came the burying and covering with hay. In the spring I had to reverse the process, digging first through layers of semifrozen leaves, pounding with my spade to loosen the ice crystals and uncovering the rose slowly over a period of weeks. Then there were pruning and feeding and aphids and black spot and mildew to contend with. I want easy roses.

Jane Kaufman, a landscape designer and a friend of Charlie's, draws a plan and gets us started. She is full of good ideas. She knows of an easy rose, a miniature called a Fairy rose, that forms masses of color against shiny green foliage and requires no burying and unearthing. She starts talking hemerocallis and physostegia and allium and acidanthera, and after a while, I am throwing back words such as tangutica and anthemis and achillea and loving the sound of the Latin words as they roll off my tongue.

One day I go to a lunch for a newcomer to the city. The conversation touches on gardens, and I begin showing off, bringing up my Latin names, extolling the virtues of my Fairy roses, pretending, in fact, to be far more knowledgeable than I am. Someone tells how she once had thirty roses on which she had lavished care and many hours, but which perished when the new owners of her house, who had said they loved gardens, proceeded to tear them all up. The conversation moved on to the kinds of things new owners of houses do to the things old owners have cared for and loved. I sit on both sides of this fence and feel a little guilty about it. I drift off a bit. After a while, the guest of honor turns to me and asks, "Do you have Sonia?"

Who is Sonia? I think, rapidly trying to order my thoughts and mark the place I started to drift off. Maybe the cleaning person someone was discussing earlier. "No, I don't," I reply, "but I've heard she's very good."

My questioner looks at me oddly. "Such a lovely color, don't you think? Soft, like a seashell."

Now it is my turn to stare uncomprehendingly.

"The rose, the rose," she says. My ignorance is exposed. The only roses whose names I know are Peace and Queen Elizabeth.

But I do know from books on Victorian architecture that the Victorians left the foundations of their houses bare, so that the whole structure was visible. Architects did not build with concrete blocks in those days, and the foundations of their houses were generally constructed from irregular blocks of whatever stone could be locally quarried. Since they wanted their houses to relate to nature, that local stone was supposed to remain visible, just as it was in outcroppings in the surrounding area.

Victorians preferred their flowers and plants away from the house, often encircling some focal point, such as a fountain or gazebo.

We have neither fountain nor gazebo, but we do have a large stone bird bath. At Jane's suggestion, we move it to the front yard and circle it with some hosta taken from the current foundation plantings. Jane also wants to plant salmon-colored canna around the bird bath, saying they are very Victorian. My aunt says that the only place canna belongs is in a graveyard, and in truth, a graveyard is the only place I've ever seen them; but we will plant them anyway and see what happens. We can always pull them out if they're too funereal. Where Roald built the wall forming the terrace and front porch, clumps of cement and grout and general grinding have left but a few scraggly spirea, or bridal wreath, but there are masses of overgrown hosta along the north side. Jane and her helpers move the majority of this hosta to bare areas under the maple and apple trees in the back yard, leaving just enough for a narrow low border at the base of the wall. With the exception of two small junipers that guard the front steps, we will let the stone wall remain visible as in the old days.

In the process of moving all these plants around, we disturb the area where last fall the children had buried the remains of their pet guinea pig. "Watch out for Henrietta!" they shout, flying out of the house to surround the bewildered workman who is loading up his wheelbarrow. "Where is Henrietta? What did you do with her?" They poke and prod at the dirt. I try to discourage them, fearful that they will uncover something ghoulish and gelatinous, but there is nothing. Perhaps Aggie got Henrietta, too.

Some of the plants we are moving are the peonies on the

south side of the house, the plants that last summer disintegrated under the onslaught of the layers of old sheet metal and asphalt from the south deck. Their roots are still intact, and small red shoots are pushing up through the crumbs of cement and bits of glass that still litter the area, so we think they will have a chance somewhere else. This whole area on the south side of the house remains a disaster zone. Mud City, we call it. Nothing much is growing there. When it rains, water courses through it, sometimes running down into the window wells and dampening the basement. Aggie has a heyday in the mud that is left.

But this is the logical area for a small vegetable and herb garden; the plants can avail themselves of the warm south sun, and I have only to step out the kitchen door to harvest. Jane has a brilliant idea. Why not pave the area with large flagstones, removing one every now and then and planting clumps of herbs in the open spaces? Three raised beds with a fourth along the fence will take care of our vegetables. The water can run off over the flagstones; there will be no more mud, and I can walk around among my herbs and vegetables snipping away like a monk in a medieval monastery garden. This garden turns out to be my favorite. To accommodate the water run-off, the stones are set so that they make a series of little steps, and when it rains, there is a tiny waterfall, a little rill. A large pot of pineapple sage sits on the top of these steps, and a small one of marjoram faces it at the bottom. We have sage and summer savory, dill and thyme, tarragon, oregano, mint, salad burnet, and rue. In the vegetable beds are spinach, beets, lettuce, arugula, and, of course, chives and parsley. Still to go are tomatoes, cucumbers, and pole beans, which I'll plant at the end of the month. Next year sugar snap peas can go along the fence along with the beans. I feel very lucky to have this disaster area turned into such a jewel.

We open the pool and once again the ducks come in for a landing. A robin builds a nest we can peer into from the stair window. All of us watch her progress daily and are rewarded by the sight of three yellow beaks waving around as two exhausted parents shove chewed-up worms down open gullets. Kate and Chris are fascinated. They use binoculars to see more clearly, and Kate tries to take a picture. Both children are thriving on this more relaxed pace, and I hope we can keep up the good spirits through the summer's construction. Chris is a devotee of T-ball, a very junior version of baseball which eliminates the hazards of pitching by six- and seven-year-olds by substituting for the pitcher a vertical rubber tube that holds the ball just at the batter's level. Everyone gets to hit and run, and sometimes to catch and throw. Chris has joined a neighborhood team and trots off three days a week to Kenwood Park for practice or a game.

Kate has decided to give a party to celebrate the end of school and, incidentally, her half-birthday. She invites twelve friends for swimming, games of the water-filled-balloon type, and hot dogs. I can see this will not be a decorous sort of creamed chicken and peas little girls' party, so I haul out the picnic table and paper plates and open the basement for the girls to use as a changing room. I am right; there is a minor food fight and some spraying with the hose, but nothing out of the ordinary until after dinner, when I suddenly hear shrieks coming from the basement.

"Blood, blood! There's blood on the door!" I rush to the basement, sure that at least one of the guests has met with catastrophe. Three of them surround me, tugging as I reach the foot of the stairs.

"Is it true? Was she really locked in there? And that's her blood? Kate says it's her blood on the door. And her claw marks! There are bloody claw marks on the door!"

They are, of course, referring to Mrs. Pruitt's door, the story by now embellished and exaggerated to include the possibility of werewolves. I reassure them that what they see is not blood, only the wood showing through the paint. "No, those are not claw marks, only hammer marks," but, "Yes, someone once was locked down here." The horror of the story is diminished, but not erased. One of Kate's friends stays to spend the night after the others have left. As I pass by my daughter's door, I hear the friend saying, "Don't you think it's awful, to have shut the lady in like that?" and Kate's voice, saying soothingly, "My mom says that maybe it was kinder. She would have to be tied up, put in cold water. They didn't have tranquilizers then."

"My mom says. . . ." Never in a hundred years did I think I'd hear her say those words again.


## June

Chris has already been at day camp for a week when I wave good-by to Kate, on her bus for camp. It is with mixed emotions that I send her; letting go of the old things and launching a bird who is ready to fly are two parts of the same thing, bringing both joy and regret. I have such admiration for her independence and derring-do, such sadness at beginning the long process of loosening the bonds, such nostalgia for my past self at this first venture off alone, for Kate is going to the same camp I went to. I know she will have a wonderful time, but I will miss her.

I don't have much time to dwell on these things, however, because Harold has already arrived at the house, and I walk back into a whirlwind of activity. Last night Charlie and I moved most of the furniture out of our bedroom. Now three bureaus line the hall, leaving only a narrow path, and we can't turn around in the laundry room at all, for all the tables and headboards and lamps piled there. Our clothes are tightly packed in Kate's and Chris's closets, where they will have every opportunity to wrinkle themselves before we put them on. All that remains in our bedroom are the two mattresses and box springs on a steel frame, and Harold is already at work unscrewing the bolts when I walk into the room. He has recruited Art to assist him. There is something very familiar about the scene. Two heavy leather carpenters' belts lying on the floor, prickly with hammers and screwdrivers, tape measures and nails, Harold and Art hunkered down over some project on the floor, arguing about the best way to proceed — in this case, whether to pile the mattresses in the center of the room or lean them against the walls.

I am not sure it's nostalgia I feel, but I laugh anyway, glad to see them both. Harold has formed his own company and has built an entire house and a garage since I last saw him, in addition to helping with a restaurant remodeling and restoration job downtown. Art has been in medical school and for the summer is working part time at a nursing home, part time in the carpentry and Sheetrock business — no longer his first loves, but they do pay the rent.

We spread out cardboard first, then heavy canvas drop cloths to protect the floor. I, more knowledgeable this time than the last, run for the masking tape and secure the edges to the floor molding, knowing that the canvas sheeting will have to withstand plenty of tugging. All the while we are performing these tasks, I am getting caught up on our friends of last spring.

Susan is getting a divorce, I learn. I knew it was in the offing. She is sad, but relieved that a decision has been reached at last and very busy with contracting and painting work. Frank, the German sculptor, did indeed return to his native land for the birth of his child. He is living on a North Sea island, connected to the mainland only by a train that ran two times a day, a train that became the labor room and nearly the delivery room for his newborn son. Paul married the nice, sweet girl who used to come to pick him up from work. He is still in the carpentry business and still working with Susan.

We did not call Susan in on these small jobs because we can handle whatever minimal amount of subcontracting is necessary — some electricity for the kitchen, a small extension of the floor. For those small jobs, a knowledge of structure and history, of how the Victorians built their houses, of whether their engineering was adequate or inadequate is not necessary. However, I am a little uneasy about our arrangement. Susan was a big part of the work we did last summer. I came to rely on her, and besides, we are hiring the very carpenter she brought in. On the other hand, it is foolish to pay a contractor's fee for a job we can handle ourselves now that we've learned enough from her to do it!

We end by piling the mattresses in the little sitting/dressing room off the bedroom, so that the carpenters can work, unobstructed, when they are replacing and taping the new ceiling. Art and Harold set up their stepladders, unsheathe their hammers, and go to work. Crash — first one chunk of plaster, then another, falls to the floor as the old ceiling begins to give way. Clouds of dust rise from the debris. Harold and Art put on surgeons' masks. I flee, choking. The ceiling is down in an hour, but the remains are not removed until the end of the day.

Trash can after trash can of heavy, dusty plaster goes up and down the stairs. We are in a mess — the stairs, carpeting, furniture covered with plaster dust — but in an infinitely smaller mess than we were in with sandblasting.

The next day, the new ceiling is in place. Fantastic. Sheetrock is certainly easier to work with than plaster. On the third day, Art brings in long stilts that he attaches to the bottom of his feet and begins taping up the cracks between the pieces of Sheetrock. How amazing it is that he can balance on those things. They have no handles like the stilts we played with as children; besides, Art's eyes are focused upward on the ceiling, and he is manipulating a trowel and a tray of plaster. I remember Charlie and me standing on makeshift scaffolding in our old house putting up the ceiling wallpaper that kept falling down. There is certainly something to be said for expertise.

By the time Art has finished the ceiling, Harold has finished the closet. Instead of heavy doors that slide off their tracks, we have louvered folding doors and new casings and decorative corner blocks that match the rest of the room. That we had to remove those two carved crowned blocks from a window in the basement is no loss. The window had been filled in when the downstairs bathroom was added, a modernization we certainly do not want to undo.

Harold moves to the kitchen to work on the little eating area we want to construct from part of the back porch. The first thing he does is to dig down right next to my vegetable bed, the one that holds the tomatoes, to pour a concrete pad, or footing, for the corner of the porch that never had one. Victorians were not big on footings, as we learned last winter, watching our chimneys going up and down a bit, the cracks forming on the walls. With the footings in, and only a pile of rubble remaining on the grass, Harold moves into the kitchen itself and starts to knock down part of the wall that separates the kitchen from the back porch. This year I am prepared. I know what is going to happen. Chaos. I ask Harold to put up a sheet of plastic, stretched from the ceiling to the floor, just inside the wall that will go down. In addition, I drape sheets of polyethylene over the counters and stove every day after breakfast, then roll them up again when I have to make dinner. Cleanup is minimal. Oh, there are still muddy floors, boot tracks, a few nails; but nothing like last year. This we can live with.

Charlie and I have also worked out a system, of sorts, for dealing with the daily questions that come up during construction of any kind. We write notes to each other. Someone will have a question: Do we want to use the old window in the mud room area of the porch, or do we want it set in the wall that separates the mud room from the eating area? What about the height of the window? Two inches make a difference. Outlets? Where and how many? Which of the outside lights will we control from the kitchen panel? I'll write the questions down and give them to Charlie in the evening and get the answers. The next morning, Charlie will be back with *his* list of questions: How many switches can the wall panel accommodate? If we use a small window in the wall, will it have weights or will it open with a crank? Will we need a steel beam for support? Are the joists sufficient? In an old house, one never knows the answers before actually uncovering the part to be worked on. Like a surgeon performing an operation, one does not know exactly what one will find. We think at first that we will have to use a steel beam for support, but discover that if we don't mind an extra jog in a wall, our current structure is sufficient. Charlie used to try to tell me his questions instead of writing them down, but he has learned that if at 7:00 A.M. I am still groggy enough to pour coffee into Chris's cereal, I will never be able to remember the details of his questions. So he writes them down, and I get the answers during the day.

We also have a business lunch together about once a week during these construction periods. That way we don't have to argue in front of the children, who also benefit from our lack of preoccupation, and I get lunch at a fancy downtown restaurant! Further, the tension level is considerably lower this year than last. We do not have the nasty financial surprises that took us unawares last year, as the carpenters each day discovered more and more rotten wood. This year no one has to deplete a savings account.

Harold has a new helper now, a young man named Todd — broad shouldered, strong, quiet, and good with dogs, which is always an asset around here. That Todd and Aggie should get along so well is indeed fortunate, because Aggie is up to her old tricks again. She gets Todd's lunch today, and I don't even hear any cursing, just "Oh boy!" and then "Aggie! Aggiieeee! Come here!" In spite of today's theft, Aggie is better. Age has made a difference. There are actually hours now when Aggie wants to sleep, and she seems to have channeled her energies into something constructive, like retrieving balls. Besides, we recently learned that a squirt gun filled with vinegar is more effective than dog biscuits in getting her to behave.

Harold has spotted some carpenter ants, seeing more of them as he gets deeper into the structure of the wall. He warns me about the possibility of a nest hidden behind a big beam he is going to have to remove. He has found some damp wood. Some rot back up in the corner is a strong possibility. I don't think much about it until suddenly the beam is dislodged, and it is raining ants. There are millions of them, crawling all over our shoulders, in our hair, ears, everywhere. We brush them off frantically, in terror and revulsion. A disgusting-looking mess of pinkish white eggs and larvae falls on the ground, right in the midst of Harold's tools. Ants cover his toolbox and leather belt. I grab the can of Flit and start spraying madly and wildly. Harold and Todd rush the beam off to the dumpster. When Harold returns, he sees me with the Flit. "What are you doing? Stop that!" he shouts. "I don't want that stuff all over my tools!" Harold is concerned about the toxic effects of the insecticide on his tools and hands. To me, those are minor considerations considering the alternative of leaving those squiggly, wriggly pink things; but no matter.

I throw the Flit on the ground and start running again because Harold and Todd have left the gate open and a strange dog runs into the yard and jumps on the floating blanket covering the pool. He falls in off the edge, clambers back out onto the blanket again, and falls in again on the other side, gasping and choking. I manage to pull him out and am now left with a six-inch scratch on my leg. Was I really talking harmony and peace, everyone happy at his work?

Once the wall is down, things move quickly. I hear the vibrations of drills, the whine of saws — no lullaby, but not intrusive like last year. Harold constructs the wall that will separate our new eating area from the mud room on the back porch. This wall is of necessity rather odd, thick at one end to accommodate a large supporting beam and the many electrical connections, thin at the other to fit between two of the five casement windows we are installing where before there were screens. In this way, we can keep the porch's appearance on the outside very much as it was before. The change is visible only on the inside, where we will extend the existing chair rail around our new eating area and paper above it with the navy-and-white dotted paper we have used in the rest of the kitchen. We will do whatever wallpaper and painting are necessary a little later, when Chris's room is ready to go. The paper hanger can do our room, Chris's, and the kitchen all at once.

A new electrician named Al comes to hook up the wiring for the eating area. "While he is here," says Charlie, "why not install a couple of outlets in the living room?" Why not, indeed? Because it violates rule number one: keep the mess confined to one area, for one thing, and it points out clearly the maxim that whatever you do in an old house will take twice as long and cost twice as much as you plan. Al is here for more than a week working on the living room outlets. I have plenty of time to learn that he is an herbalist and even to sample a few of his recipes while he is drilling, and drilling, and drilling, trying to get through the ancient, huge, almost petrified beams that underlie the living room floor. The electric outlets in the living room might as well have been made of solid gold, not brass.

Upstairs we are stripping wallpaper in Chris's room and painting the woodwork. The ceiling canvas is a little wrinkled, and we think we might remove it too. Four hours after we pull if off, two huge chunks of plaster crash to the ground, one landing right on Chris's bed. Thank heavens he wasn't in it! This accident sets me spinning like a top. I lose my cool and begin racing about mindlessly. It is 5:30 in the afternoon. Charlie is in Chicago and can't help. We now have to put up a whole new ceiling in that room, a ceiling we hadn't planned on. It will take an extra four days, and Kate is coming home very soon, and we need to be out of her room. Art, who will hang the Sheetrock, can only come tomorrow, so tonight I have to move every item of furniture out of Chris's room (and where it will go, I do not know, since we are already using all available space on the second floor), move all his tiny models and toys from his room to the third floor, measure the room, figure out how much Sheetrock we need, buy it at a discount store in the suburbs, the only one open until 9:00, and somehow tie it to the top of the car. Not to mention cleaning up all the plaster that fell. I have just come back from the Super Valu, where I raced up and down the aisles searching for garbage bags, tears streaming down my cheeks. Some days are just not worth the effort it takes to get through them.

## *July*

Kate is home and Chris is still sleeping in her room, much to the consternation of both. But the acrimony is far short of what I anticipated. Kate is a different person from the ten-year-old I put on the bus just four weeks ago. Her month away has given her a sense of independence and a wonderful desire to cooperate. She wants to help all the time. "Can I empty the dishwasher for you, Mom? Can I set the table? Can I cook dinner?" I am tiptoeing on eggs, unwilling to disturb this awesome state of affairs by noticing *too* much, being gushy, overly enthusiastic.

Loren Seeley, the wallpaper man, is busy putting up the wallpaper in our bedroom. Our furniture sits huddled around our bed, like wagons around a campfire, so that Loren will have space to work on the walls. The wallpaper is a light blue-green, its stippled design taken from a type of painting done in the last century where the paint was applied with a sponge. Almost solid in color, with lots of texture, it is a good base for the stencil that will go above it. Loren is very quiet and efficient, a true master of his craft. It was he who papered the hall and living room last year and painted the woodwork downstairs. Always neat and clean, he covered everything with drop cloths, never spilled, never tracked paint around, always cleaned up at the end of the day. He worked with his two sons, big strapping redheads, extremely polite and quiet, silent, deferential, the antithesis of the rock-and-roll painters who worked on the outside of the house. If the Seeleys came on Saturday, we would invite them to lunch. Charlie and I were both impressed by the demeanor and bearing of the whole family; they were professionals.

Then, last winter, I read a short notice in the paper. . . . A motorcycle accident. A nineteen-year-old killed. His last name was Seeley; the address matched. I knew it was Loren's son. I sent him a note then, but this is the first time I've seen him since the accident. He arrived today alone; his other boy is in school. As we talk, over the next few days, he mentions that he is looking for someone to help him, someone whom he can train who would like to stay in the business for a while. Did I know of anyone? Any of the painters we employed last summer? He refers only obliquely to his tragic loss. "I had a little setback last winter, and got behind," is all he says. I want to reach out, comfort him in some way, this man who stands so alone with such dignity and asks so little; but a name is all I can offer him.

"I remember one painter who was always neat and meticulous, who took pride in his work. An artist, he has a studio downtown. He may be just who you're looking for." Just as I go to the phone to call, the doorbell rings. It is Mike, the painter we had to fire because of his sloppy work. He is back from Texas, looking for a job. Not him. No way. I tell him we are having a quiet summer, but if I hear of anything, I'll let him know. Loren gets a chuckle out of the coincidental timing, and he is pleased when I tell him the young artist, Steve, is interested in talking with him.

A friend of ours calls one Sunday from an antique show at the Minneapolis Auditorium. "I've found something you should look at," he says. "A marble-topped Eastlake Renaissance bureau with mirror and shell carvings on the top. It is in good condition. The price isn't bad." Charlie and I drop what we are doing and jump into the car. We do not want to fill our house with Victorian furniture, make it into a museum, but a few pieces here and there add charm and fit in with the style of the house. I have already got a roll-top secretary desk with burled walnut veneer from my grandmother's attic. She could not understand why I wanted "that ugly old thing" any more than I can understand someone's valuing the pink-flecked, padded, plastic-and-chrome dinette sets of the 1950s. Such is the value of looking at things fresh, out of context, sometimes. I will always see the stuffing coming out of the pink dinette chairs where the plastic was ripped, always see the table piled high with school books, a few puddles of spilled chocolate milk. I will never be able to focus on the design, see the dinette set as an object. Always it will remain the grungy utilitarian everyday piece of furniture in the kitchen of my childhood. So it was, I suppose, with my grandmother and the desk. An unnoticed object of her childhood. Certainly nothing to admire. She put it away up on the third floor and used it for storing sheets.

I imagine it takes a generation or two before what is associated with the old and drab and gray can be revisited and seen again as if it were new, capable once again of telling us things,

things about the values that created it. The Victorian desk, for instance, says something about solidity. Nothing fragile, it will not rock, cannot be pushed over. The hand carvings, the unique moldings, the care with which it was made, say something about individuality. The use of woods, the highlighting of the pieces of burled walnut into focal points, the curves and flowing lines say something about the Victorians' relationship with nature, as do the curves and flowing lines of this house. Late Victorian house colors themselves were like those of a muted autumn. The dinette set is just the opposite. It speaks of love of manmade materials, mass productions, the commonality of man. Maybe our grandchildren will ooh and ahh over the dinette set. Not I.

Our friend was right. The Eastlake bureau is indeed a gem. It, too, has a secret compartment. What looks like a piece of molding is more than that. A slipper drawer, I think they called it. We deliberate for a day, then decide to buy. The bureau fits perfectly in between the two front windows in our bedroom. It even looks like the one in the 1894 photographs.

Our bedroom is finished, except for the stencil. It is lovely now in the summer, with the tall windows open and the breezes passing through. One of the windows goes right up into the wall above, and this window we use for a door to go out onto the front deck, the porch roof, now rimmed with Harold's heavy curved railings. It is not sunrises with croissants and café au lait that we see, but sunsets; and they are glorious, the lake sparkling like diamonds. We also watch the joggers. There are many of them, for Lake of the Isles is no longer a local preserve, frequented only by the neighborhood, but an urban park, and people come from all over the city and the suburbs to jog its three-mile perimeter. Joggers come in all shapes and sizes

— some tall and athletic, springing along as if they had wings on their feet, like Mercury; others, more earthbound, huffing and puffing, doing a kind of shuffle. Some are bowlegged, some knock-kneed, some have elbows pumping like wings. Others do a peculiar strutting gait called race walking, which makes them resemble water birds trying to run on land. Where the bridle path used to be is now an asphalt strip, built specifically for the use of people on wheels, mostly bicyclists and roller skaters. People walk babies and dogs. I saw one man reading his newspaper while his Great Pyrenees dog walked him. People come to feed the geese. One kind-looking old lady appears every day with her bag of bread. She hisses like the geese, neck outstretched, when children or dogs come close enough to drive the geese away.

Parts of it are still wild, this urban lake, and some people still come to immerse themselves in nature as they did one hundred years ago. The two islands are wildlife preserves, inhabited by birds and turtles and raccoons. People fish, catching carp and sunfish and an occasional bass. Flotillas of canoes cover the surface on a weekend afternoon. I walk Aggie, too, bouncing along like the rest, loving this bit of nature so close, wonderful willows whose layers of bark drape themselves around the trunks like trails of Spanish moss, the leaves that open like tiny accordions in the spring. And I love living in this house. The children have privacy and so do we. It won't be too many years before Kate will be having teen-age slumber parties on the third floor. I can see them there, girls popping corn, girls plastering their faces with goo and three shades of make-up, cutting hair until the early hours of the morning — or running down to the basement room, where a Ping-Pong table now replaces the paint cans of last summer. And all the while, Charlie and I will be sleeping undisturbed in our bedroom on the second floor. Maybe.

Now the children play hide-and-seek, running up and down from the third floor to the basement. Chris decided to hide in the secret compartment the other day, and lo and behold, he found a genuine treasure, one of the special little bags of chocolate that Charlie regularly squirrels away in secret corners. Charlie is not too pleased with Chris's discovery, but it sure makes up for the Easter bunny's gaffe!

### August

We are two weeks late with the kitchen, but now, finally, it is finished — that is, except for the crowned corner blocks that anchor the door and window frames. These blocks are identical to the ones in Kate's room, the blocks we cleaned with dental tools, but they are missing now, probably gone for firewood like the rest of the door and window casings. We can't remove any more corner blocks from the basement, and thus face the prospect of making them ourselves, five years of whittling and carving on cold winters' nights. But it is not to be. Our luck holds. Perusing a catalogue from a firm in Colorado called the Silverton Victorian Mill Works, we see pictures of some crowned corner blocks, not carved, not quite right, but close; and since we are going to be vacationing in Colorado this month, we decide to put Silverton on our itinerary and take a look.

### Colorado

Visiting the mining town of Silverton is like taking a journey back in time. We decide to take the narrow-gauge train from the relatively low-lying town of Durango, up through the mountain gorges to Silverton, which sits at a height of 9,273 feet. The only means of reaching Silverton one hundred years ago, this railroad was completed just five years before Mr. Douglas built our house. We think it a fitting way to travel in our search for the materials to restore it. The train is a true old-fashioned one, with eleven cars, some with open sides, and it has an engine with a real cowcatcher and a funnel shaped like a chef's hat which belches clouds of white steam. All aboard! The conductor blows his whistle, and we clamber hurriedly up the steps.

The train moves slowly through a broad river valley dotted with small ranches. Every so often, whenever the train climbs a bit, or the wind changes, clouds of sulfurous black smoke, blown back into our open car, envelop us. The smell, coal smoke, reminds me of why people wanted so much to get out of the city and into the fresh air of the country a century ago — even though the cities were very small by our standards. Climbing in earnest now, the train begins its ascent up the side of a granite cliff, whose walls still bear indentations left by the dynamite used to blast through the huge rocks. The scenery is magnificent, the sky open above. I feel unfettered, free to soar like a hawk. At an alpine meadow, we stop to let some campers off and wave good-by to them as they start up the trail, their backpacks high above their heads. I feel as if I am really living one hundred years ago, and I expect to see at the stop, not the campers, but a gentleman in a straw boater riding a high-wheeled bicycle.

Suddenly the canyon widens, the land grows flat. We are at Silverton. The town lies on a plateau nestled in among green-sloped peaks. *True Grit* and *How the West Was Won* were filmed around here, and I can see why. Muddy and unpaved, the streets make wooden sidewalks not just a decoration, but a necessity to keep our feet out of the puddles. Victorian fake fronts abound, some restored, some not. Before we search for the Victorian Mill Works, we have lunch in a former saloon whose fake basement walls, trap doors, and secret entrance attest to its days as a bootleg bar. At the restaurant, we look up the address. When we come to 852 Reese, I think we have made a mistake. This is no millworks, no woodworking factory, but a decrepit old house. Victorian, yes, but only the diamond and fish-scale shingles on the roof gable tell us that. Old and drab, and brownish green, the house is connected by a wooden side-walk to the one next door, which is faced in false yellowish brick siding.

I knock tentatively at the door of the first house. After a few minutes, the door is opened by a blond man in wire-rim glasses who appears to be in his early thirties. "Yes, this is the Victorian Mill Works," he says. It is? I can't believe it. Where is the fac-tory? The only thing mechanical I can see is a grinding machine. No corner blocks. The man explains that this house is his office. The house next door is the factory, and soon we see that indeed it is. The back of the second house has been extended to seventy feet, and all the lathes and machines and lumber and special cutting knives are there amid walls decorated by a whole year of *Playboy* bunnies. In the middle of one wall is a series of pigeonhole shelves that hold our corner blocks. We can order them with or without carved rosettes or bull's eyes, with crowns or not. The crowns have two points versus our three, but they are close. We order fifteen. George Crane, the proprietor, has been in business since 1977. He wanted something to manufac-ture, saw a need, and started the Victorian Mill Works. Nothing sentimental. Now he is so successful he has bought a five-thousand-square-foot warehouse in Durango and plans to move his operation there. "Winters here are too hard," he says. "The snow comes halfway up to the roof. It's pretty depressing from February to June. The streets just get narrower and narrower." So he leaves for Mexico, or the Caribbean in the winter — a luxury that wasn't available one hundred years ago.

## September

We are ready to get started on the garage, the Dream Garage, one of the main reasons for our buying this house, though it seems to have gotten lost for a while. Charlie has been thinking and planning for months. The garage will go on top of the hill at the rear of the lot, above the flower garden and opposite the present garage at the alley level. Regrettably, we will lose two nearly defunct apple trees, but they would have gone soon from old age anyway. Charlie originally wanted to build a big garage on the site of the present one, where the old barn used to sit, the barn that is visible in the 1910 photograph of the house, with the horse standing in the driveway. Charlie wanted to restore that driveway and build a two-story garage, the lower story being accessible from the street. But to do that requires a cut in the curbing lining the parkway that runs in front of our house. This parkway, a mere bit of a dirt road when our house was built, is now one of the prides of the city, and the park board, which controls such things, will not let us do it. I am just as glad. To my mind, a driveway there would have been intrusive, yet another slash in the green bank, already broken by our front steps and those of our neighbors. It was different back in the old days when the next-door neighbors were a block away.

So instead of one 4-car garage, we will have two 2-car garages, the new one going into the far corner of the lot. Our lot is not quite straight, the angle of the farthermost corner being more than ninety degrees, and to make full use of the space, that corner of the garage will not be square. The odd angle presents design problems. Harold will build the shell, but we call in an architect to cope with that angle and to make sure the proportions and style of the building are in keeping with the house. He gives the roof a steeper pitch than usual and adds a cupola. He also suggests that we face the foundation with limestone where it shows against the hill, thus tying the garage in with the rest of the house. A brilliant idea, we think.

Now it is Charlie's turn to be excited. He has plans, for a hoist, for a workshop, for storage. He has saved kitchen cabinets from our old house, and one set from this one; they will work perfectly as tool holders and work surfaces. He digs out the paint remover and once again begins stripping paint — on a smaller scale this time. When he finishes that job, he gets frames and matting for his favorite old car photographs, planning to give the garage a homey touch. His garage will have electricity, water, a gas heater, and a stereo. He is happy and industrious, working on all these things.

Progress on the garage itself is extremely rapid. One day a cement truck comes roaring in; the slab is laid; we put our initials in the corner. Over the next week, Harold and Todd put the framing up. The siding, windows, and roof that matches that of the house take two more weeks; then the automatic door arrives, and the carpenters are finished. One rainy weekend, Charlie digs a small trench from the house to the garage and unrolls some copper tubing and black plastic pipe and lays them inside the trench. These will serve as conduits for the water, gas, and electric wires. Al, the electrician, comes once again and drills and drills and drills; this time it takes him two days and a diamond bit to make it through the two-foot-thick limestone blocks that form the foundation of our house. The connections are made, and the garage lights up like a pumpkin on Halloween.

Now Charlie can begin work in earnest. He spends his evenings stuffing insulation between the two-by-four studs on the walls of the garage or nailing foil-backed pillows of it to the roof beams. We see two of our old pals again: Roald comes back to do the limestone facing, and Art finishes the walls by taping the Sheetrock. This time there are no hitches, or hardly any. Art inadvertently pulls down some wires Charlie has carefully installed for his stereo; and Charlie and I clash briefly over the issue of an intercom. I want one. He does not. We compromise on a telephone, which he promises he will answer, so I don't have to go out into twenty-below-zero cold to call him to the phone. I also remember from my own heyday of telephone play (Do you have Prince Albert in the can? Well, let him out!) the number to dial to make our own phone ring. If Charlie does as he promises, the system should work very well.

A neighbor gives Charlie an old Victorian screen door with spindles in a row across the middle. Together with two windows overlooking the lake, the door makes it seem that the building is an artist's studio, not a garage at all. That is, until the cars arrive. For a few days, they are glorious in their new home, freed from their mildewy prison. Charlie piles in children and friends and takes many trips around the lake. Then he starts taking the cars apart, and now the poor old Lincoln is but a passenger cab and a chassis. The fenders, bumpers, and entire engine are dispersed about — on and over the floor, ceiling, and cabinets.

## October

The geese are very noisy today, squawking and honking and practicing their V flights in small groups of about ten or twelve, back and forth across Lake of the Isles, a training session for this year's crop of adolescents. None too soon. For though the air is warm, the trees have lost a fair number of leaves, and the ground underneath them is looking more yellow than green.

We, too, are preparing for winter this year, by installing a furnace that works, one that will not run up gas bills that will make us paupers before we finish the house. So, while Eric, the neighborhood handyman and painter, puts the final touches on the new garage, three burly men chop apart three thousand pounds of old iron boiler, coating themselves and everything around them with soot in the process. But not the upstairs. This time I know. When the furnace man tells me there might be a little dust, I shut every heat register in the house and cover them in Saran Wrap. I even anticipate, with a shrug of my shoulders, the gates that will be left open for Aggie's escapes, the workmen who will be tramping all over the house. In this case, they are measuring heat loss in every room. I don't dare ask for the results of their figures.

Susan is back, thank heavens, dealing with the things we forget, such as making sure the furnace people fill in the pit where the old furnace sat and relabel the ducts so we will be able to control the airflow to various parts of the house, and making sure the three burly men don't knock out any necessary support posts and do replace the bridging when they move ducts. In spite of Susan's efforts, the job takes four days instead of the two anticipated. I tell the men they are really doing very well, all things considered. They are used to working in relatively new houses, and the housing codes to which they must adhere were written for such houses. An air intake, for instance, is very important in a house that is fairly airtight. In one with constantly circulating breezes, like ours, it is not so necessary. Yet we have to have it, and the men have to put in another three yards of duct work for this modern-day code.

The furnace men cannot run the exhaust out the chimney either, as they had hoped. Our chimney is offset, which means that the flues inside do some curving around. The code won't allow exhaust in offset chimneys, so the pipe has to be outside, on the side of the house, and it has to be eighteen inches above the ground, and we can't count window wells. Placement of the exhaust duct, therefore, becomes a problem. Where and how and how to hide it — behind a pine tree, as it turns out. Susan is her inimitable self. Six places at once, cajoling, praising, urging everyone on. Her hair is shorter; strands of gray are beginning to appear. She still gets down on the floor and plays with Aggie. It is good to see her again.

## November

There are two areas of the house we haven't tackled yet — the third floor and the front vestibule — and it is amazing how quickly and easily we slide into the decision not to do much about them for a while. This time there are no pushes and pulls, arguments about to what extent to renovate, how far to go, no shoulds and oughts. It would be nice to restore the third floor to its former glory as a ballroom, doing double duty as the library/family room it is now. It would be nice to have glowing floors, oriental rugs, the kind of curtains that would show the beautiful windows to their full advantage. But we are at the stage now where the children eat popcorn in front of the third floor TV, where they wrestle and tumble over the backs of two squishy chairs that fold out to become mattresses. Sometimes they throw spitballs. If we were to have shiny floors and oriental rugs, the rugs would be crumpled and wadded as if ten dogs had tried to make their beds in them, and the floors would be crisscrossed with marks from electric train tracks.

A leak in the third-floor bathroom, though, needs attention. If anyone takes a bath and splashes, the water comes through the floor into the laundry room below, right on top of the clean-clothes basket. Unfortunately, the ancient linoleum that covers the bathroom floor extends out into the hallway, where it lies *underneath* the red wall-to-wall carpeting that covers the stairs, the hall, and most of the third-floor ballroom. To do a proper job, we would have to rip up the carpeting and remove the linoleum; then, of course, once the carpeting was off, we would be on to ripping off the rest, redoing floors, and so on. For this one time, we decide not to do a proper job. We will leave the red carpet in place and put some new linoleum only in the bathroom; and we won't even do that until next year sometime. If the clean clothes get a little wet in the meantime, they'll dry.

As far as the front vestibule is concerned, we will slowly and not too diligently continue our search for the proper doors. Looking for them can be a sort of excursion yielding serendipitous results. On one trip to a salvage company, we wander past iron fountains and giant plaster-of-Paris Junos and Venuses basking in the last warm rays of the autumn sun, into a sort of shed that holds an acre of doors, none of the right size or quality; but there are some pretty stained glass lamp shades, and we find just what we need to replace the fern that currently hangs over our kitchen table dropping bits of itself into our food.

Novembers in Minnesota are unpredictable, and the warm sunshine soon yields to a fury of snow and sleet. We have a bona fide ice storm, one that leaves every twig and branch glinting with a coating of ice so thick that the branches make a clicking sort of music when they touch.

Lake of the Isles looks like the kingdom of the Ice Princess, breathtaking in its beauty — snow covering the ground; the lake, as yet unfrozen, still sparkling blue in the sun. All over the city, however, those same lovely ice-coated branches have been leaning on power lines, and consequently, we have no electricity. The first night isn't too uncomfortable, nor is the morning. Our gas stove still functions. But during the day, the temperature drops rapidly. I turn on the burners on the stove, open the oven door, light fires in all three fireplaces and keep busy frantically running from one to the other with boards and bits of wood from the piles of scrap lumber that still line the basement hall. Charlie is out of town, which makes things difficult because I don't know whether to leave the house and drain all the pipes — how do you drain all the pipes? — or stay and try to keep the temperature above forty degrees.

In the end, we stay. I go and fetch my eighty-year-old mother-in-law, who has neither electricity nor stove. We cook and eat by candlelight, while the stove blasts away. We will all sleep in Kate's bedroom, where I have got a roaring fire going. We have sixteen candles and two old French Pigeon lamps, little brass kerosene lamps that somewhat resemble miner's lanterns. Kate's room is brilliantly lit, cozy and cheerful, and we have a wonderful time telling ghost stories and talking about great-grandmother's séances. We even sing some camp songs, such as "Around the Blazing Council Fire Bright" and, my old favorite, "Wishcraft." At 2:00 A.M. I go down to the basement to get wood for the fire. I am *freezing*. To think that people actually

lived this way, that for the first twenty-three years of its existence, the only light this house knew was the kind we had
tonight! Of course, it wasn't so cold. There was some sort of
heating system from the beginning. Still, it boggles my mind.
When the truck from the electric company finally appears in the
alley the next afternoon, with an apparatus to knock the
branches off the power lines, I run out and nearly hug the
driver. One night was enough. We could not have stayed another.

## December

This year we have Christmas at our house, the turkey and the
trimmings, all the relatives, the works. Dream and reality, fact
and fantasy can combine this Christmas, for this is the perfect
house for such a celebration. My fantasy fifteen-foot tree stands
majestically in the stairwell, all lighted and draped with green
and gold beads and crisscrossed with popcorn and cranberry
chains. It is dressed in trinkets, some handmade by the children, from dough and paper, others collected over the years.
Fourteen of us have gathered today, cousins, grandmothers,
aunts, and seven children, and it is no trouble at all. We sit
around the warm living room with its palm tree and look of a
conservatory to open presents. After the last exclamations of
joy have died down, and the last bit of paper has been thrust
into the fire, I pause for a bit and think about how this house
works. The adults can talk to each other; the children play with
their new toys in the old second parlor, now an open area, or
in the hall, or upstairs. The dining room is just large enough to
hold the Christmas dinner table, which is fully opened for the
occasion, with three leaves. A fire in the now usable fireplace

makes the room cozy and very special. Food and dishes, turkey and plum pudding, and the inevitable rutabagas slide easily in and out of the dining room via the pass-through into the kitchen, located next to the area where the former dumbwaiter carried beef roasts from the dark and grimy basement stove to the serving area.

I wonder if the early occupants of this house had as much fun as we are having today. In a celebratory mood, we toast each other with Christmas wine. I think about how similar in form, but how different in tone, this Christmas dinner is from those leaden Sunday dinners of my childhood. This, I think, is one of the rituals that has kept its meaning, this time of new beginnings. I think, too, of the ghosts of Christmases past, the Pruitts and the Regans and the Douglases and the Kellys. Perhaps they are standing behind our chairs clinking their glasses as we raise ours, for we have indeed taken our place in the parade of lives that has moved through this house. I think about how the past shapes the present. We can make our present lives as if there were no past, building them on top of the buried past as if we were building a new city over an old one. But once the past begins to be dug out, excavated, the new structures on top are threatened, begin to topple — civilizations, cultures, individuals, and houses. Our house was threatened, remodeled without regard to its past. In uncovering it, and restoring its integrity, we discovered bits of our pasts, too. We dug out our own Pruitts and found our own Regans. Our own tears, our own laughter, our own failures and triumphs are now a part of the history of this house.

After dinner we go skating. We put on our skates in the front hall (miraculous, after years of trekking to the warming house) and skate out onto the frozen lake, just as the occupants of the house did nearly one hundred years ago, when the lake held a racetrack for trotters pulling sulkies, as well as a rink for skating; in the days when Clydesdale horses hauled huge blocks of ice from the lake to be stored for summer cooling. We skate out onto the lake and glance backward over our shoulders at our lighted, wedding cake house, now a fantasy afloat in the growing darkness. It seems to be smiling at us.

TH
3401
.C47
1986

Chrisman, Katherin

Dreaming in the
dust

 22 1988

MAR 2 1 1992

LIBRARY
FASHION INSTITUTE OF
TECHNOLOGY
227 WEST 27TH STREET
NEW YORK, N.Y. 10001